MEXICO'S REVOLUTION

Then and Now

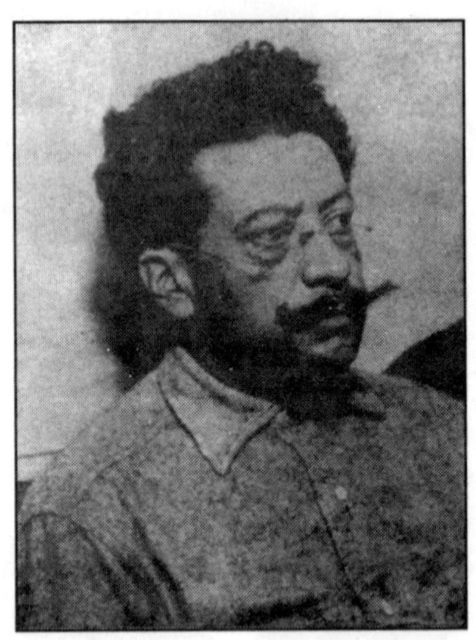

Ricardo Flores Magón (1874–1922),
early anarcho-communist revolutionary.

MEXICO'S REVOLUTION

Then and Now

James D. Cockcroft

MEXICO'S REVOLUTION: Then and Now
James D. Cockcroft

First Published in India 2014

ISBN 978-93-5002-310-5

Published in agreement with Monthly Review Press, New York for publication and sale only in the Indian Subcontinent (India, Pakistan, Bangladesh, Nepal, Maldives, Bhutan & Sri Lanka)

Published by
AAKAR BOOKS
28 E Pocket IV, Mayur Vihar Phase I, Delhi 110 091
Phone : 011 2279 5505 Telefax : 011 2279 5641
aakarbooks@gmail.com; www.aakarbooks.com

Printed at
Sapra Brothers, Delhi 110 092

Contents

To Rosario Ibarra de Piedra

Acknowledgments

I began my research into the intellectual precursors of the Mexican Revolution during the 1960s, when I was visiting and defending political prisoners in Mexico's Lecumberri Prison. The prisoners and the precursors inpsired me. This book represents the synthesis of a lifetime of research dedicated to my beloved Mexico. It would be impossible to cite all the workers, peasants, students, and academics of Mexico whom I have learned so much from, and continue to do so. I would like to extend my gratitude to the following people: Elvira Arellano, Saúl Arellano, Heather Dashner Monk, Héctor de la Cueva, Ross Gandy, Angel Guerra, Rosario Ibarra de Piedra, José Jacques Medina, Edgard Sánchez, and Marta Sánchez Soler; the workers and hunger strikers of the Sindicato Mexicano de Electricistas (SME) and the Miners' Union, for their militancy and contributions to my understanding of the labor situation; Guadalupe Ortiz and Jorge Cleto of Jorale Editores/Orfila, who published *Precursores intelectuales en el México del siglo xxi* (2010), a Spanish language version of this book; Michael Yates, Martin Paddio, Scott Borchert, at Monthly Review Press, and copyeditor

Erika Biddle, who encouraged me and patiently awaited the delivery of these chapters; and finally, indexer Elliot Linzer.

To my friends in Canada, the United States, and Latin America who supported me by accepting my self-imposed leave of absence from my usual tasks of solidarity and human rights work: many thanks, *merci beaucoup*, *muchas gracias*, comrades!

On a more personal level, a special appreciation for countless acts of help and joy go to my family and grandchildren—and especially to my bilingual good girl upstairs, Maya Marley Bickell! To my colleague and best friend, Dr. Susan Caldwell, whose acute perceptions on the themes of gender, race, and class continue to enlighten me—you provided emotional support when I was overwhelmed with working on this book, helped keep me on an even keel, and our morning talks still enrich my life more than words can ever express . . . a big hug and, yes, a smile of victory!

INTRODUCTION

Precursors and Revolutionaries ¡*Presentes!*

Almost half a century ago, during a sudden downpour in Mexicali, Baja California, I took refuge in a worker's home. Over coffee we talked about the economic difficulties caused by the high saline content of the Colorado River water flowing into the Mexicali Valley. I plunged into this struggle to correct the problem and was the first author to expose it in respected U.S. publications.

After finishing our coffees, my new friend showed me the contents of an old trunk his grandfather had left him many years ago. In the trunk were articles, letters, and other documents of the "Magonistas," the Flores Magón brothers and their allies in the Mexican Liberal Party (PLM). Dating from the early 1900s, these papers fascinated me. Thus was born my interest in the PLM, the Magonistas, and the "Intellectual Precursors of the Mexican Revolution"—the title of my first book in 1968 (reissued in 2010 by the University of New Mexico Press). Its Spanish translation, originally published by Siglo Veintiuno Editores in 1971, is currently in its twenty-fifth edition.

Back then, I was waking up politically. I developed an interest in analyzing contemporary anti-imperialist struggles and defending human rights and quickly realized I would have to research history in order to improve my participation. Now, in this centennial year of the Mexican revolution, intellectuals and activists interested in Mexico are turning their attention once more to the roots of the Revolution. Those roots show up in the strikes, military actions, and ideologies put forth by the so-called revolutionary "precursors," mainly the Magonistas.

Of course the Magonistas were revolutionaries who played an important role in the Revolution of 1910–1917 and in this sense were not only "precursors." Moreover, the roots of the Revolution were in many other movements, leaders, and individuals—from the times of Miguel Hidalgo y Costilla, José María Morelos, and Benito Juárez to the years of Francisco I. Madero, Francisco "Pancho" Villa, and Emiliano Zapata. In this sense we honor the year 2010 as the bicentenary of the declaration of Mexico's independence from Spain and the centenary of the Revolution, all in the spirit of recovering historical memory in order to contribute to the resolution of current social problems and the construction of a new "people's power"; that is, a truly participatory and transparent democracy with social justice and full national sovereignty.

As many researchers and authors have shown, the Magonistas shaped a movement that clearly articulated the pressing issues of the new century: human rights and the roles of the original peoples (often called Indians in Mexico) and the peasantry, women, immigrant workers in the United States, workers, and the immiserated masses—unemployed, underemployed, and overexploited. These issues are of extreme importance in our current century. They represent an historical continuity in spite of the technological advances and changes in social structures that have taken place.

Of equal relevance is the Magonista treatment of the roles of the state, the clergy, repression by military and paramilitary forces, nationalism, and internationalism. All these elements are absolutely fundamental for any analysis of the most difficult situation that Mexico's peoples faced a century ago—and still face today.

Without a doubt, Magonista ideas of anarcho-communism, mixed with a strong dose of socialism, resonate today. As the famous novelist and ex-political prisoner José Revueltas once put it: "the revolutionary activities of the Magonistas are the starting points of the Mexican working class's socialist consciousness—one of its own, national."[1]

This is the context in which I offer this book, as a bold but humble contribution to current debates. The first chapter examines the similarities and differences between two decades separated by a hundred years—the first decade of the last century and the first decade of this one—and their popular uprisings. The second chapter establishes the international context: imperialism and its use of the concept "failed state"; the new wars; and popular resistance. The third chapter presents the historical context: uneven economic development; the shaping of a unique political culture; the state and the formation of social classes; and clientelism. The fourth chapter reveals the genocidal terrorism of neoliberal capitalism, with a focus on NAFTA, underemployment, and the destruction of families. The last chapter investigates migration; human and Nature's rights; *politiquería* (politicking); and popular resistance movements on the eve of the local elections of July 2010 and the presidential elections of 2012. In the conclusion there is a brief discussion of the salient factors in the ongoing debates on how to reactivate the revolutionary struggle in Mexico in the face of a worldwide economic and climate crisis, and in the context of the Revolution's historical lessons and legacies.

CHAPTER ONE

Mexicans Rise Up, 1910–2010: Similarities and Differences

> If what they want is martyrs from Cananea, here they're going to find them, in the doorways to the mine.
>
> —JESÚS VERDUGO, strike committee president, Cananea, February 15, 2010

To understand the strengths and weaknesses of multiple generations of popular movements against the economic system and its power elites in Mexico and achieve a more profound historical analysis, we must uncover several of their shared characteristics, always in an international context. This chapter will compare the two periods 1900–1910 and 2000–2010.

The Revolution of 1910–1917 was an explosive confrontation between social classes that pitted peasants and workers against landlords and capitalists. It was marked by intense nationalism, that is, a challenge to the economic and political interests of the imperialist powers, especially the United States, whose investors controlled 14–20 percent of the land in Mexico.

Whatever the internal class and ethnic divisions may have been, when the revolutionary struggles erupted from their social bases, all the fractions of the "modernizing" bourgeoisie and the "traditional" oligarchy agreed on one thing: the need to defeat the peasants and workers and prevent the lower classes from conquering the upper classes definitively. In this sense, there was no social revolution, only a political one, and even that political revolution was less complete than is customarily assumed. The social struggles have continued, with their ups and downs, until today.

The Constitution of 1917 proclaimed a supposedly "revolutionary" capitalist state with a strong presidency, which, as it turned out, required years of internal and external struggles to become consolidated. There were many competitors for state power, but almost all who triumphed were big boosters of manipulating revolutionary rhetoric for capitalist ends. President Lázaro Cárdenas (1934–1940) introduced a profound nationalism, but he never intended to break with the capitalist system. Carlos Salinas de Gortari (1988–1994) and his successors were servants of foreign capital, criminals and thieves on a grand scale, who sacrificed national dignity (*dignidad*)—a hugely important concept in Latin America connoting self-respect and pride—on the altar of their own greed and the economic and political interests of Mexico's giant neighbor to the north, the United States.

In the first decade of the twenty-first century, situations remarkably similar to those of the first ten years of the previous century have reemerged in Mexico. Among the recurrences are: economic crisis; corruption and divisions among the elites; an overwhelming influence of foreign capital; fraudulent elections; labor strikes and international fights for labor and human rights; increased militarization; guerrilla attacks; new political parties and anticapitalist ideologies; waves of migration; massacres, tortures, and imprisonments of activists; blocked upward mobility, and often downward mobility, for the intermediate classes[1]; and an immiseration of the masses accompanied by an incipient loss of fear among the populace in the face of state repression.

At the beginning of the twentieth century, Mexico had a "modernizing dictatorship" entering its twilight years of power, during which many of its citizens were unemployed or obligated to work in the United States. Today, as another supposedly modernizing dictatorship enters its final years, nearly a third of Mexico's labor force is unemployed or working in the United States, where more than 41 million Mexicans and their families reside. Some 12 million of them do not have legal papers and survive under increasingly difficult and terrifying conditions.

Today the authoritarian system does not have a leader like Porfirio Díaz, frequently reelected as president, but small powerful groups who share the presidency, always at the beck and call of big capital, foreign and domestic. To maintain their power, they use fraudulent electoral processes, disinformation campaigns trumpeted by the mass media, clientelism, corruption, and above all, violence by military, police, paramilitary, and narcotrafficking forces. All these forces share political power more completely each day, whatever their internal conflicts might be.[2]

These ruling groups consist of handfuls of individuals, interconnected but fighting among themselves—businessmen, narcotraffickers, military officers, and political leaders, principally from the PRI (Institutional Revolutionary Party) and PAN (National Action Party) but also former PRI and PAN members who now form the major part of the leadership of the PRD (Party of the Democratic Revolution). Most are corrupt, and all accept and serve the neoliberal system of contemporary capitalism and economic integration with the United States under terms that are disastrous for the nation, echoing the situation during the "*porfiriato*" (thirty-four-year reign of Porfirio Díaz). Blathering about "the new democracy" that enables more than one party to win the presidency, they practice the old dictatorship of capitalist interests.

The catastrophic results of this are evident. Mexico has become a militarized society known around the world for its violence. Its economy is in free fall, with the second most unequal income distribution in the Americas after Haiti. In the last twenty-five years the Mexican minimum wage has been the weakest of all in Latin America.

It is not surprising then that today, just as during the first decade of the previous century, a social volcano is boiling up. In 1910 Mexico had an economy that still had not recovered from the impact of a recession three years earlier. Peasants, Indians, and women were seething with anger against the violent abuses they were suffering and the losses of their lands and communal rights. Urban proletarians were becoming increasingly anxious about their miserable salaries and work conditions and a staggering rate of unemployment and underemployment in an atmosphere of growing violence, militarism, and paramilitarism, all in a nation gravely threatened by U.S. intervention. Mexicans on both sides of the border were rising up in anger.

Isn't this the situation today? In recent years, Mexicans have been rebelling more and more against their desperate economic situations and state repression, protesting the continuous presence of soldiers, paramilitaries, and policemen in their towns and cities. They have been organizing in various parts of the country at levels of self-discipline and *dignidad* (dignity) that are truly impressive. For example, the May 2006 revolt by residents of San Salvador Atenco, twenty miles outside Mexico City, blocked the construction of an international airport. Also in 2006, the peoples of Oaxaca commenced a nonviolent uprising and created the self-governing "Commune of Oaxaca" that electrified the world. The neo-Zapatistas' equally inspiring creation of autonomous municipalities in Chiapas have survived military encirclement. Following from the examples set by the armed struggle of the Magonistas[3] and Zapatistas, women have been participating more than ever and assuming leadership positions.

Mexico's peoples have also been self-organizing immense street demonstrations. In 2001 the nation's original peoples trekked, by foot and bus, from the trails of their remote villages to Mexico City's main thoroughfares for "the March of the Colors of the Earth." To protest the electoral coup d'état of 2006 that stole Andrés Manuel López Obrador's popular victory, the people of greater Mexico City carried out a three-month-long "popular assembly and vigil" in the main streets of the world's second largest metropolis. The new slogan became "Effective Suffrage, No Imposition," a slight modification of Francisco I. Madero's "Effective Suffrage, No Reelection" (ironically Díaz's motto in 1876, but one that the Magonistas introduced in the first years of the twentieth century through the popular revolutionary newspaper *Regeneración*, the "independent newspaper of combat"). On December 4, 2009, to commemorate the ninety-fifth anniversary of Francisco "Pancho" Villa's and Emiliano Zapata's entry into Mexico City, independent trade unionists, teachers, students, and *brigadistas* (brigade members loyal to López Obrador) peacefully engineered "the taking of Mexico City."

Each day Mexico's peoples direct their frustration and outrage at the economic system and its spokespeople. A growing number of Mexicans cite Article 39 of the Constitution of 1917, which grants the people national sovereignty and "the inalienable right to change or modify the form of their government." Many voices in the popular resistance movements, including López Obrador's, are calling for the founding of a new republic with full national sovereignty.

That is exactly what the revolutionaries of a hundred years ago sought and, despite their divisions and defeats, achieved on paper if not on the ground in the 1917 Constitution. Influenced by the Magonistas, it was at the time the most progressive constitution in the world. In order to deepen our historical perspective on contemporary problems, a brief review of the Magonistas' political analysis and practice can be quite illuminating, especially with regard to the roles of the original peoples and the peasantry, women, immigrants in the United States, workers, and the unemployed, underemployed, and overexploited masses. Of equal importance is the Magonista approach to the role of the state, the clergy, military and paramilitary repression, nationalism and internationalism.

THE ORIGINAL PEOPLES AND THE PEASANTRY

The original peoples of Mexico and all the Americas have experienced colonialism and imperialism as an uninterrupted process of 518 years of genocidal subjection and enduring resistance. This process has entailed ecological destruction, the creation and perpetuation of an unpayable debt as a tool for economic blackmail and domination of a people, and the routine use of kidnappings, disappearances, torture, and violence against women.

The Magonistas understood the suffering and dignity of the original peoples. Ricardo Flores Magón and his two brothers, Jesús and Enrique, like Benito Juárez, grew up among them in Oaxaca. The Flores Magóns' parents, who had considerable Indian blood, maintained traditional, communal, customs.[4] Flores Magón and the PLM emphasized recognizing the rights and cultures of the original peoples and all of the peasantry. Many women and men from the peasantry and the nascent proletariat joined the political, economic, military, and ideological fights of the PLM, from the big strikes of the first decade of the twentieth century to the key military victories that forced Porfirio Díaz to sign the "peace treaties of Ciudad Juárez" and leave the country in 1911.

The Yaqui Javier Buitimea and the Mayo Fernando Palomares were Magonista leaders in Sonora during those years. Later, the young lawyer Antonio Díaz Soto y Gama, a PLM veteran, became a key adviser for Emiliano Zapata. During the Aguascalientes Convention of 1914 he crumpled the Mexican flag in his fist, asserting that it symbolized "the lie of history" since "our independence was no independence for the native race, but for the Creoles alone," a sensational challenge that brought leveled pistols before his chest.[5]

Primo Tapia, a Purépecha from Zacapu, Michoacán, began his political life as an emigrant to the United States, where he became a Magonista and participated in the Industrial Workers of the World (IWW) after it was founded in 1905. He returned to Mexico in 1919 and led revolts in various states, thereby forcing their governments to distribute lands to the original peoples but also earning the hatred of the authorities and the hired gunmen of the large estate owners. After joining the Communist Party of Mexico in 1921, he helped organize the National Peasant League (1926), but was captured and died under torture the same year.

In 1905–1906, the PLM proclaimed a revolutionary ideology opposed to imperialism and in favor of the workers, peasants, and progressive elements of the bourgeoisie and intermediate classes. Thousands of Mexicans united behind their cause. On July 1, 1906, the PLM printed half a million copies of its program, in which it emphasized the importance of the original peoples and the need for radical agrarian reform. Most of the program's points were more revolutionary than the Zapatistas' "Plan de Ayala" (November 1911) or the Constitution of 1917. Point 48 of the program guaranteed "protection of the Indian race."

The "exposition" of the program and Point 50 stipulated "the return of the *ejidos*[6] to the peoples who have been stripped of them . . . especially to restore to Yaquis, Mayas, and other tribes, communities, or individuals the lands of which they have been dispossessed." Also, by calling for a complete agrarian reform and not mentioning indemnity for the expropriated lands, the PLM program was the most revolutionary of the epoch (and in this regard today as well).

Points 28, 37, and 47 of the program exemplified its revolutionary character. The first proclaimed, "All debts of rural day laborers to their employers are hereby declared null and void." The second said, "the state will either create or develop an agricultural bank that will lend money to poor farmers at low interest rates, payable in installments." The third provided for "measures to eliminate or restrict usury, pauperism, and scarcity of basic staples."

The program even had a "special clause" on not paying the national debt, very relevant during the economic crisis that so oppresses Mexico and other developing nations now: "The Mexican people do not want any more debts burdening the Fatherland and therefore will not recognize any debts that the dictatorship, under any form or pretext, thrusts upon the Nation, whether by contracting loans, or by recognizing, too late, previous obligations which no longer have legal value."

In his famous essay, "To the Proletarians,"[7] Ricardo Flores Magón explained why there were so many economic points in the PLM program. "To be effective, political freedom requires the presence of another freedom," he wrote, "economic freedom." The rich "enjoy economic freedom and that is why they are the only ones who benefit from political freedom . . . therefore the program shows the measures the Mexican proletariat must take to conquer its economic dependence."

WOMEN

On September 24, 1910, *Regeneración* published a famous and controversial article by Ricardo Flores Magón, "To the Woman":

> If the man is enslaved, so are you. Chains don't recognize gender . . . the same claws that exhaust the man strangle you. . . . The frontiers of women's destiny are lost in the blackness of fatigue and hunger or in the darkness of marriage and prostitution. . . . A woman's wage is so paltry that frequently she has to prostitute

> herself in order to sustain her children, when in the marriage market she fails to meet a man who takes her as a wife, another type of prostitution sanctioned by law . . . because marriage is nothing else but prostitution in the majority of cases. . . . A woman's condition in this century varies according to her social standing, but tradition and law continue to subordinate her to the man. An eternal minor, she is placed by law under the tutelage of the husband; she cannot vote and cannot be voted for, and to be able to sign civil contracts she must possess worldly goods.[8]

The PLM, in spite of the patriarchal tendencies of many of its male members, was the only party at the time that encouraged women to enlist in its ranks as members with full rights. Many working women responded, particularly in the textile and cigarette industries, and became active militants in the strikes of the so-called "precursor era." Women became leaders in the fights launched by the Magonistas, and many of them were jailed or assassinated (as in Río Blanco-Orizaba, Veracruz, in January 1907). For example, Margarita Ortega led a Magonista guerrilla group in the northwest. Her daughter was assassinated by soldiers in 1912. Margarita herself was captured in 1914 by federal troops loyal to Huerta, tortured for four days, and finally executed.[9]

According to Enrique Flores Magón, "Our women comrades smuggled arms from El Paso" (in the folds of their clothing). In May 1911, the *New York Times* observed that "women have taken a spectacular part in the revolution."[10] A large number of these revolutionary women came from the PLM or felt inspired by it. However, Sara Estela Ramírez, Teresa Urrea, and María Talavera have received relatively little attention when compared to the women commanders of the Zapatistas, or the "women revolutionary soldiers," before the post-1917 official mythology converted them into simply the servants of men in arms. Yet these three women reflect the wide range of origins, courage, and strength of women choosing to be independent at a time when it was extremely dangerous to do so. Each of them related to Magonism and the struggles of *los de abajo* (the underclasses).

Sara Estela Ramírez, a poet, schoolteacher, trade union organizer, and journalist, was an important spokesperson of the PLM. In one of her poems she wrote: "The worker is the arm, the heart of the world." Her poem "To the Woman" shows her feminist attitude: "Rise up! / . . . to action / and powerful, beautiful in qualities, magnificent / . . . strong of energies." Like Isidra de Cárdenas, founder of the weekly *Voz de la Mujer* (Woman's Voice), she wrote articles for *Regeneración*.[11] She died in 1910 at the age of twenty-nine.

One of the most important Indian women was the northern *curandera* (folk healer) Teresa Urrea. Among the original peoples and miners on both sides of the Arizona-Sonora border she was known as "the Saint of Cabora" because of her practice of "miraculous" herbal medicine—for which the Catholic Church condemned her for heresy. She was born in 1873, the illegitimate daughter of Cayetana Chávez, a poor Tehuecan girl seduced by the *hacendado* Don Tomás Urrea. After her mother's death, Urrea went to live with her father. When Díaz sent troops to detain her in 1890, the Yaquis protected her and launched a rebellion among the mountainous peoples of Sonora, Sinaloa, and Chihuahua, the "Tomóchic War" against Díaz and his land concessions to foreigners. In their battles, which incorporated Yaquis, Mayos, and Tarahumaras, they shouted, "*¡Viva la Santa de Cabora!*" The Mexican army and the *Rurales* (Díaz's special rural police force composed of "rehabilitated" bandits and outlaws) massacred them. Many were deported to Yucatán to labor as slaves. In 1892, Díaz ordered Urrea and her father to be deported to the United States. He married again, and the house of his wife in Clifton, Arizona, became the central office of the PLM. Urrea used funds from a national tour to construct a large hospital for the sick and wounded. She supported the PLM and helped miners' families and the poor until her death in 1906.[12]

María Talavera Broussé, the companion of Ricardo Flores Magón (the PLM criticized marriages celebrated by either the Church or the Díaz government), was described by the *Los Angeles Times* as "a brilliant and bold woman anarchist who dared more than any of the men."[13] She shared with Ricardo an anarcho-communist ideology and was frequently thrown in jail by U.S. authorities.

IMMIGRANTS, WORKERS, UNEMPLOYED/UNDEREMPLOYED, IMMISERATED, AND OVEREXPLOITED[14]

The Magonistas formed their social base among workers, peasants, and poor people in Mexico and the United States, where they sustained themselves as underpaid workers like other immigrants. They organized thousands of miners, peasants, and immigrants from Mexico and other nations, especially in Arizona, Los Angeles, and other parts of the Southwest and western United States, where the word "*huelga*" was heard before its English equivalent, "strike." They fought for the eight-hour workday in the tradition of the Haymarket Square martyrs of Chicago of 1886, in whose honor May Day was founded as the International Day of the Workers.

The widow of one of these martyrs, Lucía González Parsons (otherwise known as Lucy Parsons), was a prominent anarchist. She founded the "Chicago Working Woman's Union" when the main U.S. workers' organization, the "Knights of Labor," still would not admit women. González Parsons and other left-wing trade unionists welcomed the Magonistas who sought political refuge or work in the United States. When Flores Magón and other Magonistas were incarcerated in Los Angeles, they received strong support from prominent left wing leaders, including the anarchist Emma Goldman and the socialist Eugene V. Debs.

PLM members played very important roles in the struggles of the Western Federation of Miners and the IWW. When the IWW was at the peak of its organizing influence, more than half of its annual union dues came from Mexican immigrant workers. Half of the victims of the famous Ludlow Massacre in the mines of John D. Rockefeller in Colorado (1914) were Mexicans, and many of them were women and children.

PLM members were quite familiar with the mistreatment of Mexican immigrants in the United States, in part because they themselves suffered it. In *Regeneración* and other publications and proclamations, they made frequent reference to the exploitation of Mexicans and other immigrants. Moreover, the Magonistas achieved the unification of immigrants from Europe, Asia, and Latin America in workers' struggles, in spite of cultural and language differences.[15] Concerning Mexican immigrants, Point 35 of the PLM program was revolutionary when it was first released and remains so today: "For those Mexicans residing abroad who so solicit, the government will provide repatriation, paying the transportation cost of the trip and allotting them lands that they can cultivate."

In truth, we can learn a lot from the Magonistas about organizing immigrants, the unemployed, and overexploited and unifying them with all oppressed groups and social movements internationally to launch an anticapitalist movement. The anarchist and socialist ideals of the PLM—their split in 1908 was due in part to ideological conflicts around these ideals—strongly influenced workers' fights and political struggles of the time on both sides of the U.S.-Mexico border. Magonistas were especially important in the founding of the main workers' organizations of Mexico: those of the miners, railroad workers, textile workers, electricians, and the *Casa del Obrero Mundial* (House of the World Worker), among others.

Veterans of the PLM's armed revolts filled the ranks of the revolutionary armies of the Orozquistas, Villistas, and

Zapatistas. Between 1905 and 1908 the PLM organized dozens of rebellions in many parts of the country, along with a wave of strikes that weakened the dictatorship and prepared the ground for the Revolution in 1910. Although the armed actions failed and hundreds of strikers died in massacres like the ones in Cananea, Sonora, and Río Blanco-Orizaba, Veracruz, the examples of dignity and combativeness of so many people in battle fired the imagination of many other Mexicans who proceeded to join the struggle.

Among today's 1,200 miners of Cananea and their families, oral history continues to play a big role in the unity of their resistance. Now finishing their third year of striking, the miners are ready, as were their ancestors, to die for the cause of trade union freedom and the fundamental rights of all Mexicans. They refer to the 1906 Cananea strike with tremendous pride as a key event for the Mexican Revolution. In the PLM-organized strike, 275 armed U.S. volunteers commanded by six Arizona Rangers temporarily occupied the town until their replacement by *Rurales.* It took 2,000 Mexican soldiers to crush the strike. From thirty to a hundred miners and six North Americans died in the fighting, and countless were wounded.[16]

In 1910, Ricardo Flores Magón defined the revolutionary struggle in the pages of *Regeneración* as a conflict between capital ("accumulated labor") and labor. "Keep in mind, workers," he wrote, "that you are the only producers of wealth. . . . The more you produce the poorer and less free you are, for the simple reason that you make your bosses richer and freer, for political freedom benefits only the wealthy. . . . The bourgeoisie takes advantage of your labor, your health, and your future, in the factory, field, workshop, and mine." The only solution, Ricardo concluded, was to take "from the hands of the wealthy the riches that they have robbed from us" and expropriate "the wealth for the benefit of all, without which condition human emancipation cannot be achieved."[17]

That is what the Magonistas did when they took control of Tijuana and Mexicali and organized "the Commune of Baja California" in 1911. Later, that is how the Zapatistas organized "the Commune of Morelos" under the PLM slogan of "Land and Liberty!" suggested to Emiliano Zapata by a Magonista emissary, José Guerra. Zapata, after his break with Madero, invited the Magonistas to join him, and many of them went to Morelos.

THE STATE; THE CLERGY; MILITARY AND PARAMILITARY REPRESSION; NATIONALISM; INTERNATIONALISM

The Magonistas made frequent reference in their newspapers and proclamations to a trilogy of powers: "Capital, Authority, and Church." They opposed big capital, authoritarianism of any kind (not just the state), and the Catholic Church. A PLM manifesto dated September 23, 1911, summed up their earlier affirmations in a classic anarcho-communist way: "The Mexican Liberal Party has unfurled the red flag in the field of action in Mexico, against Capital, Authority, and Church. . . . All that is produced will be sent to the community general store, from which everyone will take according to his needs. . . . The choice, then: either a new government, that is, a new yoke, or the redeeming expropriation of private property and the abolition of all imposition, be it religious, political, or any other kind. LAND AND LIBERTY!"[18] The direct takeover of the means of production by the producers, and the distribution of goods to all the people according to their needs, was not only a goal in the political proclamations of the Magonistas, but also a concrete revolutionary practice initiated in their "Commune of Baja California." It was a maximum form of "people's power."

The Díaz dictatorship used military and paramilitary repression to terrorize and dominate the population in general and the opposition movements in particular. There were many kinds of paramilitarism in a country marked by large landed estates with cruel majordomos and hired gunmen everywhere. They routinely carried out abuses and killings, as did the "Federales" of the army, the *Rurales*, and the many police forces. Torture also was a common practice during the *porfiriato*, just as it is today.

From the very first days of the Liberal Clubs in 1900–1901 when they defended the Constitution of 1857, which they described as "dead," the Magonistas maintained a dignified nationalism. They were always warning against U.S. interventionism, which they emphatically condemned as it occurred regularly between the years 1906 and 1920.[19] The June 1906 Cananea strike was directed against the racism of the owners of the U.S. copper giant Anaconda. The workers walked out in demand of an eight-hour day, minimum wage, a merit system to eliminate discriminatory hiring practices, and the promotion of Mexicans to some of the positions occupied by U.S. personnel.

The internationalism of the Magonistas was exemplary. They were the first in human history to pronounce the need for a world revolution and to begin to implement it, in part, through their fights in Mexico and the United States. North Americans like John Kenneth Turner and Ethel Duffy Turner edited the English section of *Regeneración*. In the tradition of Father Miguel Hidalgo y Costilla, Simón Bolívar, and José Martí, Point 49 of the PLM program called for the "establishment of ties of union with Latin American countries." The Magonistas were always thinking beyond Mexico, because they were fighters for "human emancipation."

Ricardo Flores Magón viewed the Bolshevik Revolution of 1917 as an advance in the world revolution. He supported it critically from his tenure in a U.S. federal prison, where he died in 1922. Ricardo wrote a letter in 1921 rejecting the Russian "dictatorship of the proletariat" because dictatorship "always is tyranny. . . . The workers in all industries, including agriculture, must arrange production for themselves, in common agreement, each one producing according to his ability and consuming according to his needs."[20]

THE RELEVANCE OF MAGONISM TODAY

Many parts of the world have witnessed a resurgence of Magonista and anarchist ideas in the last few decades. In one sense, Magonism never stopped being an important force in Mexico, as was evident in the peoples' struggles of the 1920s and 1930s and in the Magonista influence on the 1968 student movement and the guerrilla movements since the 1970s. The magazine *El Mesquite* describes Magonism as a "true subterranean tendency in our history—by its putting forth a series of claims for social justice . . . in which there burns an ardor, the conviction of historical memory—that of our people—who since long ago, with Hidalgo, with Morelos, with Juárez, call for justice and happiness for everyone."[21]

The Magonista voice is heard a lot among the new Zapatistas, whose armed uprising on January 1, 1994, in Chiapas, harkened back to the rebellions of almost a century earlier. The Zapatistas defend the original peoples who form, together with the peasantry, their social base. Zapatista women have often acted as leaders, spokespeople, and military commanders and their rejection of electoral processes also echoes Magonism. The slogan of the new Zapatistas is still "Land and Liberty." Their public pronouncements often use the exact words of Ricardo Flores Magón. López Obrador, the SME, and other forces of today's popular resistance also condemn the "bad government," a favorite term of the Magonistas.

In general terms, the anticapitalist and internationalist position of today's Zapatistas has been the same as that of the Magonistas. From the first days of their uprising, the new

Zapatistas have aspired to help end the "sacking of the world" by the forces of neoliberal capitalism. They have helped launch and even host various meetings of the new worldwide alter-globalization movement. However, although some of the Zapatista militants call for "a new socialist state that expropriates the capitalists," in most of their speeches and acts the Zapatistas avoid using the words "anarchism" and "socialism." Moreover, in the last fifteen years the Zapatistas have rejected armed struggle in an almost pacifist manner, something the Magonistas never did. As the Zapatista commanders declared during the first failed peace negotiations in 1994: "War is not a matter of weapons . . . but of politics . . . it is not only the mouth of a gun that will achieve liberty . . . other mouths must open and shout so that the powerful tremble."[22]

There appears to be some subtle changes in the position of today's Zapatistas. For example, during the first "National Political Strike" (*paro civil*) of March 16, 2010, called by the SME and its allies in the National Assembly of Popular Resistance, the Zapatistas took part in some of the local protest actions together with the electricians, the Cananea miners, and other social movements. Although the *paro civil* was limited to certain regions of the country and was repressed, the presence of the Zapatistas struggling in solidarity with the SME was a sign of change toward unifying with organizations they previously had disagreements with. From the start of its current fight in October 2009, when the military threw 44,000 of its members out onto the street, the SME had been inviting the participation of the EZLN (Zapatista Army of National Liberation).

The new Zapatistas are not the only ones inspired by Magonism. Many movements against neoliberalism cite Ricardo Flores Magón. During the 2006 presidential campaign, the mass media condemned López Obrador as "a danger for Mexico" and ignored his national tour in the years that followed. López Obrador answered with a new monthly newspaper called—no surprise here—*Regeneración*. Its first editorial included a sketch depicting Ricardo Flores Magón with the following explanation: "This newspaper is born in homage to those dreamers who gave all they had for the freedom of Mexico. . . . [It is] to break the information cordon . . . to build a movement that does not seek power for power's sake but rather the regeneration of a Mexico devastated . . . by those who have governed during the neoliberal cycle."[23]

In Querétaro, on February 5 and 6, 2010, a broad coalition of labor unions (the ones not controlled by "*charros*" serving the bosses), members of various social movements, progressive NGOs, and political parties of the center or left convoked a "Social Congress toward a New Constituent Assembly (Preparatory Meeting)." Its "Political Declaration to the People of Mexico" said: "The actions and initiatives of the new insurgency . . . seek to recover the best of our history . . . the ideals that gave birth to the Revolution . . . in order to end the neoliberal nightmare that corrodes the country and to throw out once and for all the authoritarian regime of the mafias that govern our nation badly."

In its call to the event the SME said: "The social justice goals expressed in the Program of the Liberal Party of Ricardo Flores Magón and in the Plan of Ayala of Emiliano Zapata . . . have been undergoing cancellation. The Social Pact of 1917 that created our Political Constitution is practically in shreds and now we suffer from an economic model and a political regime that takes on the cruelest and most opprobrious aspects of the *porfiriato* . . . we workers are living more and more as in the years ending the nineteenth century."

In words reminiscent of Ricardo Flores Magón, the famous defender of human rights, Senator Rosario Ibarra, has said it is necessary "to build resistance and solidarity in an organized way among working people who as always have produced and created all the wealth and each day are drowning more in misery. . . . A state unable to generate work, health, education, housing, joy and happiness among its inhabitants does not deserve to continue existing."[24]

The praxis of the Magonistas signaled the important link between labor, migration, and revolution. One hundred years later, social and international movements are struggling for a world of equality and no borders, or "*Sin Fronteras*" (the name of an organization in Chicago that defends immigrants). We can see a growing internationalism among Mexican workers, small businesspeople, students, and intellectuals on both sides of the border that evokes memories of the Magonistas. When the immigrants mobilize to protest their unjust and cruel treatment in the United States, as they did on March 21 and May Day of 2010, they receive public support from many other workers and sympathizers in both nations. Millions of Mexican and Latino immigrants and other workers filled the streets of 150 U.S. cities on May 1 in "El Gran Paro Americano 2006 / The Great American Boycott 2006: *Un día sin inmigrante* / A day without an immigrant." It was the largest workers' march in U.S. history. Strikes and factory takeovers have also merited international support. In December 2008, more than 250 members of the United Electrical Workers (UE) in Chicago occupied the "Republic Windows and Doors" factory and won their demands. Most of the women and men were Mexican immigrants.

There are clear signs of a strengthening of internationalism in workers' struggles. The first labor triumph of the new internationalism of the twenty-first century happened in 2005 in El Salto, Mexico, where 700 workers in the high-tech tire factory Hulera Euzkadi S.A. de C.V., supported by trade unionists and individuals of other nations, won their three-year-long strike against Continental Tire, one of the largest and wealthiest transnational corporations in the world. Now the workers are co-owners of their factory, together with private companies.[25]

Nowadays, the biggest labor union confederations of other countries, such as the American Federation of Labor-Congress of

Industrial Organizations (AFL-CIO) in the United States and the Canadian Labor Congress (CLC) in Canada, support Mexican workers, including Mexican immigrants in the north. On March 11–12, 2010, the World Federation of Trade Unions, with affiliates in Latin America, Europe, Asia, and Africa, participated in an International Conference of Solidarity with the SME.

Moreover, civil society's *Tribunal Internacional de Libertad Sindical* (International Tribunal of Trade Union Freedom), has created a space where Mexican workers and labor unionists can testify about how their basic rights have been violated. It has publicly denounced the de facto government of Felipe Calderón and delivered its declarations and decisions to the main international and inter-American organizations concerned with labor and human rights issues.

On May Day 2010 its final decision was read to a mass audience in the Zócalo, Mexico City's main square. It condemned the mistreatment of all workers, including immigrants in the United States. It criticized the systematic policy of the Mexican state to "curtail trade union freedom, annul collective bargaining, deny the right to strike, and undermine the fundamental human right to a decent job." Noting the "corruption, physical violence, intimidation and blackmail" used to abuse labor and "serve private interests," especially the "alarming generalization of so-called contracts and labor unions of protection," it criticized "the criminalization of social protest and the militarization of conflicts." The tribunal called for an end to impunity and rejection of the official labor reform proposal that would "further undermine the conquests and rights of the Mexican population." It spoke out against the ongoing violations of the International Labor Organization's labor agreements 87 and 98, accompanied by "other serious repeated violations of human rights: attacks on the right to life and physical integrity; arbitrary deprivation of liberty; discrimination, defamation, use of blacklists, and sexual harassment."[26]

In this year of the centenary almost all the forces calling for a change in Mexico's political and economic system are reexamining Magonista thought and the victories and defeats of a hundred years ago that revolutionaries of different ideologies and practices experienced. Many very useful and intelligent independent celebrations of the centenary are taking place, unlike the ones of "the political class" with its opportunism and lies. To be sure, there is recognition that the narco-cartels and the level of capitalism's globalization distinguish the current situation from that of the *porfiriato*, but people realize that there are strong similarities as well.

In the first ten years of the new century there are more massive mobilizations than before in defense of labor and human rights and for a true democracy. And in some parts of the country there is a challenge to "authority" not seen for many years. At the same time, there is more repression. The U.S. government and its imperialism frame the context of what is happening in Mexico and the rest of "*Indo América Latina Africana*" in the twenty-first century.[27]

CHAPTER TWO

Imperialism, "Failed States," New Wars, Resistance

> Death and pain for so many victims in the length and breadth of the country. Meaningless deaths for no reason. Unpunished deaths. Deaths and also—again—the whip of forced disappearances.
>
> —ROSARIO IBARRA, March 28, 2010

> So that drugs will not get to your children. . . . WE ARE KILLING THEM.
>
> —New slogan of the government-censored cartoon after Mexican soldiers killed two children, April 2010[1]

A social volcano is bubbling in Mexico. Nearly half the country's eligible voters showed their disgust with the country's political parties by staying away from the polls in the off-year elections of July 2010. All the major political parties in Mexico have become neoliberal and corrupt. Broad-based social movements are resisting a right-wing offensive sparked by twenty-eight years of neoliberal economic policies that have led to the country's militarization and, after the fraudulent election of Felipe Calderón in 2006, a reign of terror unleashed by his unconstitutional self-declared "war" against drug cartels involved in bloody internecine strife.[2]

Neoliberalism's economic genocide has caused countless premature deaths and generated humiliating poverty for three-fourths of the population. Many in the intermediate classes have been pushed down into the ranks of the poor; hundreds of thousands of workers have been losing their jobs, as "flex labor" and union-busting become the norm; and millions have been emigrating. State enterprises have been privatized, and almost everything, including humanity itself, has been converted into marketable commodities for the profits of big business. The economic agony of the masses has generated a growing resistance: guerrilla wars and local nonviolent uprisings.

The U.S. government looks upon these events with baleful eyes and oils its guns. After all, Mexico is the second trading partner of the United States and the third largest provider of "black gold" to the northern giant.

U.S. INTERVENTION

For decades, Washington, D.C., has been pouring military aid into Mexico. In 2008 there were 6,000 U.S. troops on the Mexican border, and in 2010 President Barack Obama decided to send in more. The U.S. side of the border is militarized, as it was before and during the Mexican Revolution of 1910–1917 and periodically since then. Drones routinely fly over Mexican soil. In the United States, video games show American troops invading Mexico.

Remember that the United States has often sent troops into Mexico. There is a long history of U.S. involvement in the internal affairs of the nation since the bloody seizure of one-half of Mexico's territory—the outcome of the imperialist war of 1846–1848.

Today a militaristic weapon is the Alliance for the Prosperity and Security of North America organized by the governments of the United States, Canada, and Mexico in 2005. The Alliance is an expansion of the Plan Puebla Panama of 2001 that aimed at the integration of southern Mexico with Central America and Colombia. In 2008, the Alliance was strengthened by the Merida Initiative/Plan Mexico, an international security treaty established by the United States with Mexico and Central America to fight narcotraffic and integrate Mexico and Central America with the Northern Command of the United States.

These plans better U.S. chances of firming up energy security: Mexico, Guatemala, Belize, and Colombia are oil countries. The plans also make it easier for the United States, Canada, and Mexico to use their arms against outside threats and, above all, internal opposition. They represent a new phase of contemporary imperialism.

What are the real targets of these plans for the international coordination and militarization of the struggle against alleged terrorists and narcos? They are aimed at immigrants, original peoples, guerrilla resistance, political dissidents, and social movements against transnational corporations taking over natural resources, including water, and causing mining pollution. These plans, financed by billions of U.S. dollars, have made Mexico a security priority for the U.S. ruling class. They serve to "justify" the sending of U.S. personnel into Mexico to take part in intelligence operations to tighten control over the populations of both nations.

Mexico faces a dangerous and complex situation. Obama's government has beefed up budgets for sending down agents of the Federal Bureau of Investigation (FBI) and the Drug Enforcement Administration (DEA), along with personnel to train Mexicans in the so-called wars against narcotraffic and terrorism, wars against "the Evil." Obama calls it that, and righteous citizens applaud him or demand even stronger measures.

Obama's government has created a new "special force" made up of armed people from police and intelligence agencies that operate in the border zones.

The FBI and the DEA have offices in several Mexican cities. In February 2010, spokespeople for de facto president Calderón admitted that U.S. agents were active in Ciudad Juárez. The number of U.S. military contractors sent to Mexico has increased during Calderón's administration. There are videos of contractors who have trained Mexican police taking part in the torture of prisoners.[3]

In 2008, U.S. involvement in Mexico took the form of that business enterprise called Blackwater. Exposed for its crimes against humanity in Iraq, it has changed its name to Xe Services. It came to "help" Calderón in his supposed war against the narcotraffic. He is fighting "the Evil," and many churchgoing Mexicans thank him for saving their children from that horrible "narcotic," cannabis.

They don't know that this war is an excuse for militarizing the nation. Only 2 percent of Mexicans read a newspaper, and only 4 percent ever buy a book. Everyone has television, and the two TV monopolies, Televisa and TV Azteca, known as the media "duopoly," are under the iron control of two of the billionaires topping Mexico's wealthy elite. The TV duopoly, a powerful propaganda machine, is a key player on the neoliberal stage saluting Calderón's war, spewing ultraconservative pap, and warning about "the danger to Mexico" posed by such honest political figures as Andrés Manuel López Obrador, the real winner of the stolen 2006 presidential elections.

In January 2010, sixteen teenagers and students unrelated to the narcotraffic were murdered in Ciudad Juárez. There, in the last two years, some 4,700 people have died violently, and feminicide remains rampant. Most of the victims have been civilians executed by paramilitary groups or military people dressed in black or wearing ski masks. In March 2010, mysterious gunmen murdered U.S. citizens associated with the U.S. consulate there.

Ciudad Juárez, the "perfect model" of industrialization by means of foreign-owned *maquiladoras* (low-wage manufacturing assembly plants) with the cooperation of *charro* (corrupt) trade union leaders and their "protection contracts," is now known as "the most violent city on earth." There, Calderón's government is working against the Juárez drug cartel. But Calderón's forces are secretly allied to the Sinaloa drug cartel, or at least are permitting its advance against the Juárez cartel.

The boss of the Sinaloa cartel is "El Chapo" ("Shorty") Guzmán, a smooth-talking *capo* who walked out of a high-security prison in 2001 after bribing the guards. It cost El Chapo a bundle of bills but he has them: *Forbes* magazine ranks him as one of the richest and most influential men on the planet. El Chapo did the old Houdini act and disappeared during year one of governance by the first political party to break the seventy-one-year-long monopoly of political power held and enforced by the Partido Revolucionario Institucional (PRI). Since 2000, the new occupants of the Mexican presidency have come from the populist Church-backed Partido Acción Nacional (PAN). Its first new president was Coca-Cola millionaire Vicente Fox. Tall, handsome, mustachioed Fox wore boots and lied frequently, but always with a showman's good-natured smile. He invited Israel's deadly Mossad to train his secret police, the Center for Investigation and National Security that works under the Presidential Coordination Office. This was done behind the backs of the Mexican people. As Machiavelli said in the sixteenth century: "Everyone sees what you *seem* [to be] but few know what you *are*." And now, of course, the duopoly's television really does reach *everyone*.

El Chapo continues to play the "invisible man" to police dragnets in Mexico. When his kind of money is flowing, nobody can see a thing. The Calderón government wants to finish off the Juárez drug cartel in favor of the Sinaloa cartel. The FBI says its "confidential informants linked directly to the narco gangs" believe that El Chapo is winning.[4] The murders or captures of powerful *capos* carried out by the army—and the navy in cases like the Beltrán brothers—strengthens the power of El Chapo nationally and internationally.

Businessman Calderón's popularity is sputtering like a bonfire in a hailstorm. Under the hail of bullets from shootouts, public opinion is beginning to snarl on all sides. When *el Presidente* walked into an auditorium in Torreón in early 2010 he was deafened by a crowd of booing citizens. The TV duopoly covering his appearance barely snuffed the sound in time.

Five transnational corporations control the U.S. mass media for imperialist interests and say nothing or spread lies about the people's uprisings in Mexico and the Mexican immigrants in the United States.[5] This is because the U.S. government is focusing its sights on the rising Mexican opposition in order to gain greater control over Mexican oil, minerals, uranium, water, biodiversity, *and immigrant labor.* And it wants to keep immigrant labor cheap, and so aligns with the Mexican business elite and its government. The elite loves Uncle Sam like kids love Santa Claus. The elite's Business Coordinating Council of big capitalists is crying for more aid in fighting the cartels, and the aid is pouring in. It does not come in a reindeer sleigh, mind you, but as Blackhawk helicopter gunships that spit fire and death.

In February 2010, National Intelligence Director Dennis Blair condemned the cartels and the violence in Mexico and Central America as the result of "failed states." Basic security has been undermined, and instability marked by crime, corruption, and "ungovernability" is growing, he asserted.[6] In the same fashionable language, President Obama has warned that the struggle against violent extremism involves diffuse enemies, unstable regions, and "failed states."[7] High officials of the U.S. government and its armed forces blather a lot about "failed states." We are told that these states are bleeding to death and only a transfusion of military intervention can save the patients. Good old Uncle Sam then appears as a humanitarian white-coated doctor leading a caravan of arms donors, contractors with torture needles, and flying gunships painted with a red cross.

The Central Intelligence Agency (CIA) has named Mexico and Pakistan the two most unstable nations in the world—they can melt down any minute. They are "failed states." So in 2009 Obama appointed his new ambassador to Mexico, Carlos Pascual, an expert in "nationbuilding" and in "failed states." Carlos is a Cuban American. He has twenty-seven years of experience in Africa, Eastern Europe, Eurasia, the Middle East, and conflict situations in Latin American and Caribbean nations such as Haiti. In the State Department, Carlos Pascual was head of the Office of Reconstruction and Stabilization. Its critics—among them Naomi Klein—call it the "U.S. Colonial Office." Klein describes Pascual as an expert in shock therapy for "failed states." Pascual arrived in Mexico City to begin coordination of the Binational Office of Intelligence. Crawling around in this pit are officers of the Pentagon, the DEA, the FBI, the CIA, and other critters of the U.S. intelligence community.[8] The Mexican government is not a "failed" state, because it carries out the tasks assigned to it by the empire's design. All of Washington's propaganda backs up the militarization of Mexico in order to protect the interests of transnational corporations and foreign banks.

The militarization is a revival of the "dirty war" of the 1970s, especially in the states of Chiapas, Oaxaca, Guerrero, and Michoacán. Now the dirty war is furthered by the presence of narco thugs and unemployed youth who, in some parts of the nation, work with top police and military officers. But there is another difference between now and the 1970s. Internationally renowned Mexican Senator Rosario Ibarra, famed for her outspoken defense of human rights, has pointed out that the murdered and disappeared are not only opposition figures and social movement activists but also "the civilian population unrelated to any political or social conflict or the narcotraffic. . . . [The majority] are executions of the civilian population, of youth, both men and women, and of the poor."[9]

Every rise in the number of deaths permits the military and Calderón to exclaim that they are "winning the war." Meanwhile, the number of assassinations and disappearances of human rights activists, left-leaning political figures, journalists, and social movement and labor activists has escalated in recent months and hardly ever is an assassin or kidnapper "found," much less charged. Amnesty International and academic experts on Mexico observe that the military often does as it pleases, and in fact it runs whole regions of the country. Or tries to do that: it has competition from some of the narco groups.[10]

In February 2010, General Guillermo Galván, Secretary of Defense, called for the armed forces to support a political reform proposal sent to Congress by Calderón. The reform gives the army the right to enter homes without warrants and arrest anyone on suspicion. Soldiers who shoot civilians "by mistake" cannot be tried in civilian courts. Bloodied civilian corpses are stacked high: they are "collateral damage" in the so-called "war against drugs." General Galván's publicly backing the political reform was an indication that the formation of a civilian-military dictatorship might be in process.

There is always the chance of a military coup in Mexico, and judging from the reception of the coup in Honduras the empire might welcome it. But there is another opinion: some retired military men in Mexico think that a few generals and admirals and an unknown number of soldiers are still uncorrupted and patriotic enough to believe in a more democratic system. This has happened several times in the history of Latin America.

The problem of the narcotraffic has to do not only with militarization, bad government, or "failed states." For decades, Washington's all-out campaigns against the narcotraffic in Colombia and Mexico, in Bolivia and Afghanistan, and in the United States itself, have repeatedly ended in failure. All the experts say so. You catch a *capo* and another takes his place; you knock out a drug route to the United States and other routes open up; the forbidden but highly profitable stuff is in the merchandise flowing to the North under free trade. There are "mules" willing to hide drugs on their persons. A family passed from Mexico into Laredo with a white plastic Christ in the back seat and sniffing dogs barked. It turned out to be a coke Jesus.

Yes, the situation has brought endless failure. But haven't the repressive campaigns really succeeded? They enrich (mainly U.S.) bankers through secret arrangements to launder drug money, while recycling phenomenal amounts of dirty money into many sectors of the legitimate economy. They also keep up huge profits in the international drug market for the exporting countries and their governments, a large part of which is recycled into the international arms market for the benefit of arms manufacturers.[11] The United States sells more weapons than all the other arms-producing countries put together. It is the world's arsenal of death.

The "failures" of the campaigns against the narcotraffic help to justify war, state violence, and massive repression. The "war against drugs" sponsored by Washington and its allies has nothing to do with national security or ending the drug traffic and everything to do with profits. It involves the forging of strategic alliances against democratic anti-imperialist governments like those in Venezuela, Ecuador, and Bolivia. The key alliance for the United States in Latin America is the chain of neoliberal governments on the Pacific Coast: Chile, Peru, Colombia, all of Central America except Nicaragua (where Washington is fomenting a "failed state")—and, of course, Mexico. The chain is made of iron: each government is an enemy of its people.

There are legal proposals cooking in the Mexican Congress that permit foreign troops to enter national territory. The United States has already set up seven new military bases in Colombia, and there is a bilateral agreement to build five more in Panama. There are U.S. bases in almost all of Latin America and the Caribbean. There are bases on Aruba and Curaçao, island nations once colonized by the Dutch, near Venezuela's oil fields. There are plans for creating a "multinational, multifunctional military base" with Brazil in Rio de Janeiro "in order to patrol the drug traffic of the region." Official documents of the U.S. Air Force have proclaimed that the new military bases "expand the capacity for expeditionary war . . . [guarantee] the opportunity for conducting complete spectrum operations in all South America . . . [to combat] the anti-American governments in the region."[12]

In the last week of March 2010, top government officials from Mexico and Washington met in Mexico City to discuss the terrifying violence in Ciudad Juárez and to work out a strategy. Secretary of State Hillary Clinton admitted that the U.S. demand for drugs and the arms smuggled into Mexico from the United States were feeding the violence of the cartels, so both governments proclaimed a "new stage" in the war on drugs: "Plan Juárez." Supposed social programs and *more military aid* make up the public part of this glitzy new plan, which will stuff the pockets of the Mexican government with $300 million. It aims to strengthen the Merida Initiative/Plan Mexico and the Northern Command's control over Mexico. The new U.S. ambassador to Brazil has called this military integration "armoring NAFTA" and so, in effect, acknowledges that behind the "war on drugs" is the aim of protecting the economic interests of big capital in the era of neoliberalism.[13]

After this meeting, during a TV interview for Televisa, U.S. ambassador Pascual boasted about Calderón's military strategy, saying "we designed it together." The secretary of Homeland Security, Janet Napolitano, admitted that at Calderón's "request" members of the U.S. Army work in Mexico in a "limited" way as military intelligence personnel. Calderón is throwing away national sovereignty by integrating Mexico with the United States.

In fourteen documents recently declassified by the Presidency of the Republic about "Plan Mexico 2030, Project of Great Vision" are the details of thematic workshops convoked by Calderón in October 2006. Plan Mexico 2030, says political scientist Gilberto López y Rivas, violates the Mexican Constitution of 1917 and guarantees the future "integral occupation of the country" by the United States. The plan programs the privatization of the energy sector, biosphere reserves, education, social security for state employees, and other public services. It calls for the repression and co-optation of social movements. López y Rivas maintains that the plan is inspired by imperialism and that Mexicans confront a "social war" disguised as a fight against narcotraffic. According to him, the aim of the plan "is to finish off the Mexican state." Journalist Carlos Fazio adds that what is happening in Mexico is a "low intensity war that combines intelligence work, civic action, psychological war and control of the population. . . . The center of gravity is no longer the battlefield as such, but rather the social-political arena."[14]

THE PRESENT SITUATION AND THE PEOPLE'S RESISTANCE

In Mexico, privatization is overrunning the energy sector. Nationalist forces, led by the independent electrical workers union, the miners, some independent oil workers, university students and workers, and a breakaway union of schoolteachers are resisting. These workers also back popular struggles against the "reform" of the labor laws. The "labor reform" would take away basic trade-union rights and open the door to unlimited exploitation of the Mexican people.

Calderón and his secretary of labor have launched an all-out war on these workers in violation of the Constitution and national and international laws. At midnight on October 10, 2009, soldiers and police seized the state enterprise Central Light and Power, throwing 44,000 electrical workers into the street. It was also a seizure of Central Light's fiber-optic network, which was later sold to an international telecommunications consortium of Televisa, Telefónica, and Megacable. Calderón did not issue a decree to "justify" such an unconstitutional military/police coup until *after* it had taken place.

On June 6, 2010, the anniversary of the 1906 massacre of copper miners in Cananea near the Arizona border that triggered armed revolts leading to the Mexican Revolution of 1910–1917, the Federal Preventive Police (PFP) seized Cananea's mines after an armed attack in which countless unarmed miners and members of their families were wounded, beaten, and arrested. For more than a thousand days, 1,200 striking Cananea miners of the national Sindicato de Mineros had been resisting PFP occupations of their communities and cutoffs of their water and electricity. In their protest of unsafe mine conditions that in the last three years have caused the deaths of more than 200 miners nationally, the Cananea miners were challenging the criminal negligence of the nation's largest mining corporation, Grupo Mexico.[15]

The union-busting offensive has provoked a wave of large street demonstrations. Estimates run as high as 300,000 people. On May 1, 2010, Mexico City's Zócalo square was overflowing with angry protestors and speakers condemning the "fascist" government, neoliberalism, U.S. imperialism, and a new "terrorist" and racist law against Mexican immigrants in Arizona. Dozens of fired electrical workers on a hunger strike were camped out in the square. There have been roadblocks, seizures of tollgates, refusals to pay electric bills, hunger strikes, propaganda brigades, student walkouts, university stoppages, national work slowdowns, strikes, and hastily convened assemblies of popular resistance. Because 2010 is the centenary of the Mexican Revolution (of 1910–1917), some leaders and workers are calling for a new revolution or at least obedience to labor laws and the Constitution of 1917.

And Mexico's hunger strikes, protests, assemblies, sit-ins, and debates go on. The civic resistance has been nonviolent, disciplined, and organized. So police and military forces have carried out acts of repression and attempted to provoke demonstrators to at least throw a stone at a car or bank window or even at them! TV, of course, reports it much differently. There are a dozen guerrilla groups operating in Mexico, but they have been quiet.

Many demonstrators see Calderón as "the illegitimate president." They accuse him of treason for having turned the soldiers into an "army of occupation." Some describe Calderón as the "most visible figure of the mafia" who is trying to create a military police state as in a coup d'état or a Colombian-style military police state. This includes the participation of the capos in the administration of society, not as "a parallel state" or a "state within the state" but as *an integral part of the state.* As Calderón himself has recognized, in some parts of Mexico narco kingpins charge taxes, impose laws and curfews, and build public support with their neighborhood social service projects.[16]

Accompanying the civic resistance within Mexico is the protest movement by Mexican immigrants in the United States. More than 100,000 marched in Washington, D.C., on March 21, 2010, to demand their basic rights. And on May Day 2010, more than a million of them, along with civil rights activists, marched in eighty U.S. cities—250,000 in Los Angeles alone. One out of five Mexican workers currently lives and toils in the United States. They face state terrorism: racist attacks, arbitrary arrests, illegal raids of their workplaces and communities, outright murder by U.S. Border Patrol agents, and destruction of their families through the deportation of parents of U.S.-born children. Since 1993, more than 6,000 Mexicans have died in the southern border area of the United States. During Obama's presidency 400,000 immigrants have been thrown out of the country *each year*, and in 2010 the number has been skyrocketing. Immigration and Customs Enforcement maintains 186 *secret* detention centers for immigrants.[17] The record of human rights violations in both countries is frightening. Amnesty International and other reports condemn the Mexican military for the use of torture, raping women, murdering civilians and shameless corruption.

Mexico's new popular protests are mainly defensive, however much they are spiced by calls for a "revolutionary offensive," a "Constituent Assembly," and "national sovereignty." Right now the correlation of forces does not favor the protestors. Why is this? There is a long history of corrupt unions and men-on-the-make in the political world, combined with clientelism and co-optation. There are divisions in the Mexican Left and many defeats. There are deep currents of conservatism and apolitical behavior in the traditional society. There has been criminalization of social movements with ever more killing of youth, leading to the introduction of the term "youthicide." There has been violence and terrorism against women and homosexuals. There is a climatic catastrophe of polluted cities and poisoned water. And there is an ongoing economic crisis: small owners wander among the tombstones of their workshops, and working people continue their grim struggle to stay alive. They have little time for political activism. And many Mexicans know that the Revolution of 1910–1917 cost the lives of a sixth of the population, so they avoid scenes that might erupt in violence.

Meanwhile, Calderón's violence against people in his "war on narcos" and the economic agony of the lower classes are starting to work against him: the government policy of installing fear may be backfiring as popular resistance continues. As the saying goes, "If you risk nothing you gain nothing." Better to risk yourself in struggle to change the system than to hang on with no money in the midst of daily murders. Of course there is defeatism in the society revealed in humorous cynical remarks like "it would be better for the United States to annex us now." But you never know at what moment the creation of fear in a society will turn into an expansion of rage and rebellion—an explosion of "popular power" organized from below. Remember what happened in Argentina in 2002, when the population took to the streets to topple a president and workers took over factories or in Honduras in 2009 when masses of people poured into the streets to resist the military coup and on May Day 2010 swarmed the capital city with 500,000 to 700,000 peaceful marchers under the banner "With Popular Unity to the Final Victory."

With or without such sudden turning points, the struggle in Mexico will be long and hard. There will have to be coordination of the fight of workers, peasants, students, women, LGBT activists, Indians, schoolteachers, state doctors and nurses, the urban poor, small businesspeople, eco-activists and, of course, the civil rights movement by immigrants in the United States. The key words are internationalism and unity, signs of which are beginning to appear. *Los pueblos unidos jamás serán vencidos* (The peoples united will never be defeated).

CHAPTER THREE

Uneven Development, Political Culture, Classes, Clientelism

Cárdenas is like the sun: He shines upon everyone but warms no one.

—Mexican saying

In your countries those that own the banks are getting richer with our debt while we are getting poorer and poorer.

—DOÑA A., owner of a small vegetable shop in Mexico City, and mother of three children, 1987

Throughout history, Mexicans have discovered that in order to achieve real changes in their lives they must carry out revolutionary struggles, at times armed, against colonialism, imperialism, and the state. In spite of impressive triumphs, such as the one that Indian and peasant guerrilla fighters achieved when they defeated the French military occupation of 1862–1867 that named Archduke Maximilian of Austria "Emperor of Mexico," there is a tragic record of rollback for popular victories, exemplified by what happened after 1867, when Porfirio Díaz established his dictatorship (1876–1910). Another example is what happened after the revolutionary defeat of Díaz and the assassinations of Madero (1913), Zapata (1919), and Villa (1923), when Mexico's bourgeois and political elites built the longest lasting single-party authoritarian system in modern times (1929–2000). Yet another reversal occurred after Mexicans carried out the "peaceful revolution" of social protests that supposedly ended the authoritarian system in 2000 by defeating the presidential candidate of the Partido Revolucionario Institucional (PRI).

Nonetheless, Mexicans continue fighting for social justice and democracy and are conscious of their earlier struggles, victories, and defeats. This is evident from the artistic part of their "political culture," since the creation of the first murals, songs, novels, and interpretive dances of the Revolution (1910–1917) right up to the current popular assemblies of the social movements.

UNEVEN AND COMBINED DEVELOPMENT

Mexicans' fights against colonialism and imperialism have been a logical response to the way Mexico's political economy evolved historically. Foreign domination of the economy has long been a key factor in the country's destiny and reflects, as well, the general law of historical processes: *unevenness*.

Bolshevik revolutionary Leon Trotsky called it "the law of uneven and combined development," by which he meant the drawing together of different stages of historical processes, a combining of separate and disparate steps, "an amalgam of archaic with more contemporary forms." Trotsky saw this law as especially applicable to those parts of the world less fully developed economically than Europe, or *unevenly developed in their adaptation of, and subjugation by, capitalist forms of production.* He concluded that the Russian Revolution, based upon a worker-peasant alliance, would *combine* stages of earlier human history, passing in a very brief time from industrial and preindustrial, bourgeois, and pre-bourgeois forms of social organization, to socialist ones. This, he said, was even more likely to the degree that other nations joined the international revolutionary process that he theorized as "the permanent revolution," that is, "the impossibility of socialism in only one country."

Ricardo Flores Magón understood the historical process of *combined* economic forms and the need to *internationalize* the revolutionary process. He realized that the Mexican countryside was not "feudal." Therefore, a "bourgeois revolution against feudalism" was not needed. That's why the Magonistas called for the immediate seizure of the means of production in the countryside and not just in the cities.

In truth, Mexico has long experienced an *uneven and combined development* of modern, capitalist forms of production with harsh and dictatorial forms of control over the population. The vast majority of Mexicans in 1910 constituted what Porfirio Díaz's development minister and general director of agriculture called "a rural proletariat"—landless peasants, working for what the two officials called "capitalist agriculture" in a system of debt peonage. Flores Magón realized the system resembled feudalism in its barbarity but not in its fundamental arrangement of the means of production.

As many historians have noted, an incipient unity between left-wing urban workers and the rural proletariat collapsed in 1915 when future President Álvaro Obregón signed a pact with Mexico City's *Casa del Obrero Mundial* (House of the World Worker) and its 50,000 members, who were suffering food shortages at the time. The pact created "red battalions" of militant workers to fight and help defeat Francisco "Pancho" Villa's northern army of workers, small landholders, and *jornaleros* (day laborers) and weaken Emiliano Zapata's southern peasant army. It tied the organized labor movement to the emergent "constitutionalist" state led by Venustiano Carranza and Obregón. And it generated a corrupt labor bureaucracy that usually sided with capitalist bosses and only occasionally benefitted the workers. The end result would be a poorly paid labor force dependent on an authoritarian and increasingly technocratic corporatist state.[1]

Three years after the signing of the pact, the Confederación Regional Obrera Mexicana (CROM), a predecessor of today's "official" state-recognized unions, was founded. Its 90,000 members were led by Luis Morones, famous for his ostentatious displays of wealth. Thus started the tradition of *charrismo*—corrupt trade union bossism that uses violence to guarantee "labor peace" and converts labor bureaucrats into capitalists. Today, 90 percent of union contracts are "protection contracts" that union members have often not even seen, arranged between the *charros* and the employers.

The last ninety-three years of Mexican history are unintelligible without recognition of the immediate results of the revolutionary upheavals of 1910–1917: a defeated peasantry; a crippled and dependent labor movement; a wounded but victorious bourgeoisie; and, for a divided people, a paper triumph—the 1917 Constitution that expressed an ideological change for the ongoing economic development of the nation along capitalist lines.

Surely these results were not the causes for which so many workers, peasants, and young Mexicans gave their lives and limbs. The true goals of the Revolution were the ones of social justice and democracy proclaimed by the Magonistas and their successors in Mexican history: Zapata and Villa; the oil, railroad, and electrical workers who obligated President Lázaro Cárdenas to act against imperialism in the 1930s; Valentín Campa, Demetrio Vallejo, Rubén Jaramillo[2]; and the political prisoners of the broad-based student movement of 1968 and every decade since who continued the Magonistas' combative tradition.

In terms of peasant and worker interests, the Mexican Revolution was not aborted or "interrupted." It was *defeated.* On the other hand, the lower classes did not lose the war for their liberation. They lost a battle, but the war continued, here peacefully, there violently, in the ensuing decades.

Formulistic explanations of the Revolution contain elements of truth but do not adequately embrace the complexity and "Mexicanness" of the events before, during, and after 1910–1917. That is why the following formulas are erroneous:

- The Revolution was a bourgeois revolution against feudalism;
- The peasants and workers lacked "political development";
- There was no leadership of a "vanguard party";
- The Revolution continued and was "permanent."

Without denying the historical and cultural roots of the current class conflicts wracking Mexico, we must recognize that the country has changed considerably since 1910, especially after 1940 when the economy semi-industrialized. Mexico continued changing after the 1968 massacre of peacefully protesting students and workers who wanted to democratize the country. A new labor militancy emerged, guerrilla fighters appeared, and the government, aided by U.S. imperialism, carried out its "dirty war" of the 1970s—with massacres, disappearances, and torture.[3] The nation changed again with the ascent of neoliberalism starting in 1982; the 1985 earthquake and people's solidarity in the absence of adequate government response; NAFTA and the neo-Zapatista uprising in 1994; the nascent narco-state alliance, narco gangland killings, and the economic collapses of 1982, 1994–95, and 2009–2010.[4]

All these changes were directly related to the complex legacies of the Revolution. One of those legacies was the state's propaganda that revolutionary changes were unnecessary because "we've already had a revolution here." This was not how some of the lower and intermediate classes saw matters. Their ongoing struggle for social justice and democracy created problems for Mexico's bourgeoisie, which contained conflicting fractions, torn between the benefits that accrued from their relations of dependence on foreign capital on the one hand, and their desire for more independence on the other. As we shall see later in this chapter, the heated class war of the 1930s forced the bourgeoisie and its state to accept some concessions to *agrarista* elements pushing for agrarian reform; to radical trade unionists in the energy sector; and to anti-imperialist radicals or revolutionaries.

After the Second World War, Mexico's ruling economic and political elites trumpeted the "*institutionalization* of the Revolution" under the one-party state of the PRI. However, their self-proclaimed "institutional Revolution in power," at the helm of a capitalist state organized along corporatist lines, was increasingly exposed as a social counterrevolution and a political dictatorship (which has consisted of two parties since 2000).

In sum, it was not the Revolution but rather the class struggle that continued. The Revolution was neither interrupted nor permanent. Some peasants, workers, and elements of the intermediate classes kept fighting for the Revolution's original goals but experienced state repression, co-optation, and clientelism. They made periodic attempts at self-organization through groups independent of the state, that is, an adjustment to the new counterrevolutionary conditions. And they continue trying to do that today—and learn from the lessons of the past.

Four important lessons of the Revolution of 1910–1917 are:

- The danger of handing over weapons prematurely and of trusting peace offers (the Zapatistas in Morelos in 1911);
- The importance of unity, and the trap of permitting the creation of an antagonistic division between the working class and the peasantry (the red battalions of the *Casa del Obrero Mundial* in 1915);

- The need to recognize and incorporate the demands and special needs of specific groups of the oppressed, such as women, the original peoples, and people of diverse sexual preferences;
- The importance of a genuine internationalism and anti-imperialism.[5]

The realization of Trotsky's law of uneven and combined development in the nineteenth and twentieth centuries created great wealth for a few but economic hardship for the majority of Mexicans, including small and medium businesspeople, despite their occasional moments of advance. The continued low-wage basis of capitalist growth both before and after the Revolution oppressed most Mexicans and, under the impact of the counter-revolution and neoliberalism, deepened Mexico's economic integration with the United States.

Since the end of the colonial era, Mexican employers had become accustomed to drawing on the availability of cheap labor power for their accumulation of capital. Combined with the domination of the economy by foreign investors who had more capital, production inputs, and technological know-how, this reliance on inexpensive labor power contributed to uneven and weak patterns of domestic capital accumulation. A large and dynamic internal market or a vigorous production of capital and intermediate goods failed to develop. Consequently, Mexico's labor-intensive capitalism became characterized by low productivity. Today, most of Mexico's manufactures, already reduced by NAFTA's onslaught of cheaper U.S. commodities, are noncompetitive internationally. Even items produced by the foreign-dominated *maquila* sector of the economy (low-wage, hi-tech assembly plants) have suffered from the recent competition of Chinese goods.

This incapacity to compete has reinforced the Mexican bourgeoisie's insistence on keeping labor costs down, resulting in a vicious circle. It has also maintained Mexico's dependence on foreign capital, be it in the period 1880–1940 when capitalist economic development was structurally based on agro-mineral exports or in the post-1940 period when changes in the forces of production and strong state support for industrial development in collusion with U.S. capital helped convert Mexico into a semi-industrialized country.

Trotsky's law of uneven and combined development helps us understand Mexico's historical "misdevelopment" and its economic failures of recent times. These failures include the exhaustion of the models of "industrialization by import substitution" and of "stabilizing development," followed by today's tottering neoliberal model that has earned the bitter nickname of "stabilizing stagnation." From the ongoing class struggles and state and imperialist interventions have come the diverse and sometimes unique characteristics of the "political culture" of contemporary Mexico and the consolidation of a "transnationalized" and "anti-Mexican" *vendepatria* (traitorous) bourgeoisie.[6]

POLITICAL CULTURE

In the past, historians of social change and revolution tended to underestimate the importance of interrelationships between ideologies, on the one hand, and popular cultures—mythology, belief systems, and the practice of rituals—on the other. This approach is more common today, in part because Latin America's original peoples have risen up so mightily in the era of neoliberal capitalism. These uprisings and new challenges to capitalist systems and European modes of thought represent, in the words of Ecuador's president Rafael Correa, not "an epoch of change but a change of epoch." They have had a worldwide conceptual and intellectual impact.[7]

In the case of Mexico, ideological and cultural factors are of particular importance. During the first half of the twentieth century, for example, the upsurge of new conceptions of the world and the discarding of parts of older ones, together with the preservation of traditions of self-defense and self-organizing among the subaltern classes ("*los de abajo*" in Spanish, the title of a famous early novel about the Revolution of 1910–1917), proved to be fundamental. The Revolution was, among other things, the world's first in which anarchist, socialist, and communist ideas inspired people of the working and intermediate classes to look toward the future, and at the same time it was a series of "revitalization movements" of collective indigenous traditions that looked toward the past, real and imagined.[8]

The formation of a "political culture" in Mexico has a lot to do with precisely this. The murals of Rivera, Siqueiros, Orozco, and other painters of the 1920s and 1930s fortified the myths of the past about the original peoples' rejection of the Spanish Conquest and simultaneously showed the faces of twentieth-century revolutionaries like Flores Magón, Zapata, Villa, Mariátegui, Martí, Marx, Lenin, Luxemburg, and Trotsky.

The ideology that was to legitimize the hegemonic project of Mexico's bourgeoisie was that of the "glorious Revolution," particularly as exemplified in the hypocritical anti-imperialist declarations of Carranza against the U.S. invasion and occupation of Veracruz (1914–1915), a time when the U.S. government was throwing its support to Carranza, or in the state rhetoric about agrarian reform, or in the constant call to all Mexicans to "unite in order to avoid a new bloodbath." Even as liberalism was the ideology of the bourgeoisie in the nineteenth century, so was "the Revolution" the ideological banner that would legitimize the bourgeoisie's governments of the twentieth century.

Also contributing to the creation of a political culture that continues affecting people's attitudes today was the apparition of the presidency as a sacred cow not to be questioned during the prolonged reign of the PRI. The clientelism practiced by the PRI and the PAN (founded by conservative Catholics in 1939 and in the presidency since 2000), as well as by other political parties represented in the Congress, further shaped the political culture. For its part, contemporary neoliberal capitalism has strengthened in Mexico, as in other nations, the parts of the political culture that are most individualist, consumerist, deferential to authority, *machista*, religious, patriarchal, sexist, and racist.

There is a "depth structure" in Mexican ideology and political culture, a remarkable continuity in style despite vast changes. In some important respects, the PRI and the PAN (or the "PRIAN" as some call it), with their operative emphasis on hierarchy and the *jefe máximo* at the top, are heirs of the *Científico-porfirista* administration.[9] Mexican politics' pyramidical oligarchic features are hardly just reflections of contemporary circumstances, but also of historical patterns of authority. The Spanish adaptation of *caciquismo* is a case in point. *Caciques* were local leaders of the original peoples, often elders, who received and merited the support of *los de abajo*. The Spaniards adopted *caciquismo* and corrupted it in their administrative system "from the top down" (*desde arriba*), giving it an authoritarian and violent dimension that the PRI later "institutionalized." Not surprisingly, most Mexicans today reject or resent their local and regional *caciques*. Another example is the Maya custom of *compadrazgo* (co-fatherhood), which readily became amalgamated with the European "godfather" system. *Compadrazgo* served as a patriarchal form of harnessing Indian labor and fortifying class hierarchy. It provided a patron-client form of exchange that expanded throughout Mexican history and remains common today. A better-off *compadre* was expected to assist his "godchild" with gifts on birthdays—and at the same time keep his eye on the activities of the peasant or worker family to make sure there were no signs of rebellion.

Almost all the norms of authoritarianism that mark contemporary Mexican political culture have their roots in the subjugation of the original peoples. Among these norms are "*personalismo*" (favoritism rendered by powerful individuals), "*presidencialismo*" (the president or leader as beyond criticism), and "*la mordida*" (bribe). These norms also reinforce an omnipresent corruption that European colonialism introduced in Latin America and the Caribbean.

Above all, colonialism deepened the subjugation of women in a religious and patriarchal system marked by extreme *machismo*. In colonial times women were viewed not only as sexual objects to be seized by force if necessary, or as workers in artisanry, agriculture, and industries like tobacco and textiles, but also as brood mares, expected to produce as many future laborers as possible. In the absence of the *generational production of labor power*—that is, women having and raising babies who grow up to become workers generation after generation—no economy can exist for long. Then as now, women's daily production of labor power at no cost to employers made huge contributions to the generation of wealth that does not appear in statistics.[10]

In the twentieth century's post-revolutionary society, *los de arriba* used the "revitalizing" and "revolutionary" elements of Mexico's "cultural construction" to consolidate a state capable of controlling the masses and also of introducing certain reforms that were required for the industrialization or "modernization" of the country, as well as for negotiating with foreign capital and for their own acquisition of wealth. But *los de abajo* also used those elements of popular culture in their fights *against* the bourgeoisie, the *hacendados* and *latifundistas* (big landholders), and foreign capital.

The Revolution dismantled an old oligarchic state. Starting in 1917, the triumphant segments of the bourgeoisie, led by the industrial-financial bourgeoisie of the North (the so-called "northern dynasty"), undertook their political project of reconsolidating Mexico's capitalist state along new lines. But during the 1920s and the better part of the 1930s, no major social class or class fraction could assert total or clear-cut hegemony. It was the type of situation that Antonio Gramsci once theorized as "catastrophic equilibrium."[11]

Mexico's victorious modernizing bourgeoisie was still a weak one, facing the more powerful U.S. bourgeoisie with its huge economic investments in key sectors of the economy. In addition, various bourgeois individuals composed a "*comprador*" fraction whose interests were tightly knit with those of foreign capitalists. Moreover, Mexico's bourgeoisie had to fight off rivals *within its own class and within the Catholic Church who were seeking to restore the old oligarchic order* (as they are trying to do today under different circumstances). Above all, the bourgeoisie faced challenges from peasants, workers, and intermediate-class radicals who were demanding implementation of the agrarian, labor, and education reforms promised by the Revolution and the 1917 Constitution.[12] For example, there were 1,289 strikes between 1920 and 1924, before a "social pact" between the CROM and President Obregón guaranteed labor peace at least for a while.

The situation was even more complex. The Cristero Revolt of 1926–1929 involved not only a conflict between the Church and the state but also a peasant uprising in the Bajío region to the north and west of Mexico City. The peasants raised the same banner they had used during the War of Independence in 1810, the Virgin of Guadalupe, in whose redemptive qualities they trusted. Other peasants took up arms to help the government put down the Church-sponsored revolt, which did not end until U.S. ambassador Dwight Morrow, a partner of J. P. Morgan and Company, intervened to negotiate a settlement easing President Plutarco Elías Calles's enforcement of the anticlerical clauses of the Constitution.[13]

It was a moment when conflicts between classes and within classes were reaching a critical point. Even the Church was divided on the Cristero Revolt. Fascist groups calling themselves "*Sinarquistas*" emerged, and by 1940 they and their paramilitary appendage, the "Gold Shirts," numbered nearly half a million.

Revolutionary peasant and worker groups also gained strength, armed at times with the help of regional *caudillos*[14] or the new state in formation.

In 1928, shortly after being elected president, former President Obregón (1920–1924) was assassinated by an obscure Catholic fanatic. The political situation became even more unstable, and this led Calles, one of the nation's largest landowners and by then the major figure of Mexico's polity, to build a more authoritarian and centralized one-party system that might manage the multiple crises better. Launched in early 1929, the Partido Nacional Revolucionario (PNR), precursor to the PRI, was the first national political party of any significant size. It managed to draw together rival parties, military officers, and *caudillos*; to give cohesion to the political, civilian, and military bureaucracies; and to "fix" national elections so that only one party could win.

However, the new one-party system, which lasted until 2000, was initially unstable. The world's Great Depression erupted later in 1929, and the intense intra-bourgeois conflicts reappeared among competing factions of the PNR. Moreover, the *agraristas* and anarchist, socialist, and communist revolutionary trade unionists were more active than ever. Much of the countryside had become engulfed in violence, with peasants engaged in a fierce war against the "white armies" of the large landowners. Often the peasants' only allies were rural schoolteachers, more than 200 of whom were shot down by the *latifundistas*' hired *pistoleros*.

By the early 1930s, class war was intensifying and shaking the very core of Mexican society and politics. The original worker-peasant goals of the Revolution once again moved to center stage. It was a time when the nation's political culture would ripen, deepen, and become more complicated than ever. It was to be the decade of agrarian and labor reforms and the nationalization of oil.

STATE AND CLASSES

After 1917, many regional *caudillos* participated in the new post-revolutionary state and soon converted themselves—along with several of the petty bourgeois lawyers, intellectuals, and labor racketeers who joined their governments—into powerful political bureaucrats waxing fat from state favors to big capitalists, both domestic and foreign. The capitalist structure of the economy conditioned state policies, with the result that the bureaucrats and *caudillos* were often able to join the ranks of the bourgeoisie upon leaving government. This informal alliance gave rise to a new political elite that became known as "the revolutionary family." Political scientist Francisco Valdés Ugalde has described them as "politicians made into businessmen thanks to the private appropriation of public money."[15]

However, in the beginning of the 1930s, the state and the contending fractions of the bourgeoisie and other political actors were structurally limited by the economy's dependence on external conditions: accumulated foreign debt; agreements with foreign shareholders; the Great Depression that tripled Mexican unemployment by 1933; and the United States' deportation of more than 300,000 Mexican immigrant workers and their families, many of them U.S. citizens, victims of a powerful eugenics movement that claimed Mexicans were a "menace," "inferior," and "born communist."[16]

The modernizing fractions of the Mexican bourgeoisie faced a resurgence of peasant revolts and workers' strikes that they could handle only with the assistance of class alliances and a strong state with a populist ideology, readily available in the state-controlled sector of trade unions, the one-party system, and the heritage of the Revolution.

President Cárdenas (1934–1940), like his predecessors in the "revolutionary" presidency, encouraged each group contending for power—businessmen, workers, peasants, schoolteachers, new bureaucrats and caudillos that had entered the state, original peoples, women, and so on—to form organizations with which the state could work. The Federal Labor Law of 1931 already had affirmed workers' rights to unionize and strike, but it also had laid the basis for state regulation of labor by granting the state the right to declare strikes legal or "nonexistent" and to recognize or void the elections and directorates of labor unions.

As an army general, a former state governor, and a presidential aspirant, Cárdenas had over the years formed friendships with several workers and peasants. Yet as minister of war in 1933 he ordered the disarming of Veracruz's peasant militia directed by socialists, communists, and anarcho-syndicalists. In this way he practically assured his nomination for the presidency and some degree of confidence from the bourgeoisie.

In his governorship of Michoacán (1928–1932) and his presidential campaign, Cárdenas promised his support not only for the common folk but also for patriotic segments of the bourgeoisie, those most rooted in nationally controlled areas of production, at the expense of *comprador* and imperialist groups. His administration developed good relations with several powerful Mexican financial groups. It fomented private enterprise by allowing the government's major development corporation, the Nacional Financiera (founded in 1934), to underwrite private investments and to provide start-up capital for industrial enterprises.

In the midst of a wave of strikes against foreign companies and serious political challenges, on June 13, 1935, Cárdenas delivered his famous "Fourteen Points" speech. He was responding to a right wing offensive that a resurgent conservatism and ex-president Calles had launched against militant unions of the Confederación General de Obreros and Campesinos de México (CGOCM, founded in 1933). Cárdenas delivered his speech in the industrial city of Monterrey, a hotbed of bourgeois reactionaries and a city paralyzed at the time by a general strike.

In his speech, Cárdenas said that many of labor's demands were reasonable and granting some of them might stabilize the economic situation, assuming that concessions to labor were guaranteed "*within the economic possibilities of the capitalist sector*." He urged capitalists "not to continue provoking agitations" like lockouts because "this would bring on civil warfare." He encouraged workers to form a "united front," which the government would deal with "to the exclusion of minority groups which might choose to continue" (for example, the CROM, loyal to Calles but superseded by the CGOCM).[17] Cárdenas also encouraged employers to "associate in a united front"—which many of them rapidly did, forming chambers of commerce and industry across the land.

The Fourteen Points speech was a broad populist appeal to all social groups with the aim of putting them under state regulation. It was a classic example of Cárdenas's populist and corporatist strategy. His administration encouraged a multitude of organizations to bargain with the state and (wherever feasible) affiliate with the national political party, granting them state recognition as legal entities yet maintaining them each separately so as to avoid, for example, encouraging unity between peasants and workers.[18]

Many industrialists and bankers welcomed increased state intervention, and even social reforms, if such measures would control the class struggle and if the bourgeoisie would gain an ally (the state) in its hegemonic project to maintain capitalism and achieve stable political power.[19] Of course, the reform project carried out by Cárdenas ran a risk: some of the ideas accompanying the project's propaganda implied a change in basic social relations and the dominant capitalist ideology—"socialist" education, for example—with corresponding instability.[20] But despite the risk, the Mexican bourgeoisie, to achieve its goals, had to delegate power (or accept, in the case of bourgeois fractions, less modernization) to the state sufficient to, in Engels's words, meet "the economic necessities of the national situation."[21]

In mid-1935 there was no guarantee that the contest would not lead to the common ruin of the contending forces or that the doors would not be opened to a more revolutionary (or counter-revolutionary) transformation of society. But Cárdenas always insisted on carrying out his reforms "*within the economic possibilities of the capitalist sector*." He had proclaimed during his presidential campaign that the class struggle was "an essential within the capitalist regime" and that his agrarian reform in a country still predominantly rural would emphasize the protection of private property and favor small private land parcels over communal landholdings.

And that is what his agrarian reform did. In spite of his distributing more than 20 million hectares, double the amount distributed by all the post-revolutionary governments before his, Cárdenas maintained and stimulated the private system of commercial agriculture. Yucatán in the southeast and areas in the northwest and the north received the most state support for *ejidos* because peasant land struggles were strongest there. But even there, Cárdenas typically left the most productive lands in the hands of large corporations and *latifundistas*, who experienced an increased production for export that contributed to a subsequent boom in capitalist agriculture. For example, in the troubled Laguna region of northern Mexico, where he launched a state-sponsored project of collective production on *ejido* lands, Cárdenas left the highest quality lands in the hands of twelve corporations, 70 percent of which were foreign-owned. The best one-third of the Laguna lands, with more than two-thirds of the artesian wells, remained untouched by his agrarian reform. Nationally, less than 10 percent of all *ejido* farmers benefitting from the agrarian reform worked on a collective basis; most farmed individual small parcels within an *ejido*.

Between 1930 and 1940, the number of privately owned farms increased by 44 percent. Some 800,000 persons were still living on haciendas in 1940, when the government acknowledged that Mexico continued to be fundamentally a country of great estates. The estimated number of haciendas was 11,470, perhaps more than in 1910, while the percentage of national territory controlled by large-scale landowners was 42 percent, compared to 60 percent in 1910.

It is no coincidence that *neolatifundismo* soon emerged as the dominant form of capitalist agriculture in Mexico. In the final analysis, Cárdenas's agrarian reform avoided more violence and civil war, while helping to increase capitalist production manyfold. Nonetheless, the agrarian reform gave many peasants a feeling of *dignidad* that they and their descendants would never forget. Most peasants appreciated Cárdenas's efforts and affectionately called him "*tata*" (Nahuatl for father).

Women also benefitted, thanks to literacy campaigns, the partial restoration of their communities, and the introduction of the home sewing machine and the *molino de nixtamal* (mill for grinding maize soaked in lime and water, the mixture for making tortillas). These new technologies reduced a woman's daily toil spent in traditional activities by several hours, not to mention her exhaustion.[22]

Cárdenas's program of social reforms, including his recognition of many of the hundreds of strikes shaking Mexico, was similar to reformist programs of other capitalist governments of the time, such as the "New Deal" reforms of U.S. president Franklin D. Roosevelt. It was a way of saving capitalism from the Great Depression that the same capitalist system had caused and to avoid the overthrow of capitalism by *los de abajo*.

Cárdenas was a nationalist. In response to the demands of rail and electrical workers he gradually nationalized the railroads and established the Federal Electricity Commission. In more than one instance Cárdenas was also an internationalist, implementing a foreign policy of national sovereignty and independence in the tradition of Benito Juárez. He opened Mexico's doors wide to Republicans seeking refugee status after their defeat by the fascists in the Spanish Civil War. In the decades after Cárdenas left office, Mexico received thousands of political refugees from Latin America and the Caribbean during the frequent U.S. military interventions and U.S.-sponsored "dirty wars." Mexico also granted refugee status to U.S. and British professionals fleeing the onslaught of McCarthyism. Mexico recognized the Cuban Revolution and never honored the economic blockade against the "heroic island," with the partial exception of the governments of the PAN in the twenty-first century that periodically tried to implement inhospitable policies toward Cuba. For example, when Fidel Castro arrived to attend an international meeting in Monterrey, President Vicente Fox brusquely told him to "eat and leave."

Perhaps Mexico's independence was best shown, together with an amazing national unity, during the period of the nationalization of the petroleum industry in 1938. Two years earlier, oil workers had launched an intermittent strike against foreign capital and "imperialism." By early 1938, they were clamoring for a nationwide general strike to force nationalization. Cárdenas accepted the petroleum companies' final wage proposal to the striking workers but was insulted by the companies' insistence that it be put in writing and by their refusal to accept a guaranteed partial share of Mexico's oil output. The companies wanted all or nothing.

So, on March 18, 1938, Cárdenas expropriated the foreign-controlled oilfields. According to one of his closest advisers on the matter, Jesús Silva Herzog, "Had General Cárdenas not nationalized the oil, his government wouldn't have been able to stay in power."[23] The companies retaliated with a "blockade" of Mexican oil sales to the United States, England, and France and applied other strong economic measures against Mexico. In 1941, the oil boycott was lifted, after negotiations on an indemnity agreement were completed.[24]

There was a massive outpouring of public support for Cárdenas's act of economic independence, including approval by the Church. Millions of people contributed whatever they could to a national indemnity fund that had been created to pay off the oil firms. Cárdenas seized this time of national unity to cut short and terminate the agrarian reform and assure the capitalists that their investments and properties would be respected and supported by the state. Later, he sent troops to break strikes by oil and rail workers.

Above all, Cárdenas further consolidated a corporatist model of social and political organization. In 1938, the national political party was renamed the Party of the Mexican Revolution (PRM). It incorporated the major mass organizations, grouped into four "sectors": labor (CTM), peasant (CNC, Confederación Nacional Campesina), "popular," and military. The popular sector consisted of teachers and state employee unions excluded from CTM, small farmers outside CNC, professionals and other groups outside CTM or CNC, youth and women's organizations, and so forth. In 1940, the military sector merged with the popular sector.

Cárdenas's agrarian reform and oil nationalization helped stabilize the class war, while his organizing of the national political party into corporatist sectors of separate constituencies helped provide the political stability needed for the low-wage industrialization policies that followed his regime. Cárdenas, and the corporatist state he left his successors, used a specific technique to maintain social peace: channel divisions among people whenever possible into organized "competing constituencies" along corporatist lines. Workers, peasants, professionals, businesspeople, original peoples, women, students, and the poor were kept as separate as possible, while class, ethnic, and gender divisions were blurred by the ideologies of populism, national unity, and class harmony.

In 1939, Cárdenas selected the moderate General Manuel Ávila Camacho, his minister of defense, to be the PRM candidate in the 1940 election, instead of General Francisco Múgica, favored by many trade unions and peasant leagues. The CTM and the CNC leadership came out for Ávila Camacho and imposed their preference on the membership. Cárdenas counted on Ávila Camacho to carry out an industrial development program in the coming years—or as he put it in his last major public address, the task of "unification, peace, and work." Incoming presidents from the PRI echoed these themes every six years.

Underlying the period of class struggle from 1940 to the present were changes introduced by Cárdenas's successors in capitalist production, a second wave of "modernization" following that of 1880–1940, accompanied by the development of an authoritarian-technocratic state eventually presided over by U.S.-educated Ivy League graduates who would introduce the terroristic nightmare of narco-neoliberalism. The state played a larger and more complex role than it had done in the "robber baron" days of the *porfiriato*. The state not only regulated labor (and to a far lesser degree capital), but it also helped create classes or class segments. It conditioned the class structure and affected class attitudes and the class struggle itself. Whether impoverished peasants, urban slum dwellers, unionized workers, low-paid bureaucrats, or influential technocrats, Mexico's social classes and groups grew, declined, prospered, or suffered in relation to the various programs of the capitalist state. In brief, the state acted as an important agent of class formation or transformation.

By 1970, the basic trends of contemporary class formation in Mexico were already established under conditions of the state's consolidation of dependent monopoly capitalism. These trends, more visible today than in 1970, were: the proletarianization of the peasantry, as well as partial or temporary "re-peasantization"; a growing overlap between different fractions of the large-scale bourgeoisie (also known as the big bourgeoisie, into whose ranks entered some of the narcos); the growth of the intermediate classes, and their increasing internal differentiation and impoverishment; the development of a sizable, low-wage industrial proletariat, with less than 15 percent of it unionized today and most of it underpaid; labor exploitation in diverse forms, including proletarianization of the traditional petty bourgeoisie; the fragmentation and atomization of the working class as a whole; the immiseration of the majority of Mexicans; and the intensification of internal and external migration.

The exhaustion of the "stabilizing development" model and its eventual replacement by the "neoliberalism" model, as well as the onset of periodic political and economic crises starting in the late 1960s, contributed to the acceleration of these trends. As production, distribution, and exchange became more concentrated, centralized, and uniform during capitalism's development into monopoly capitalism, and as imperialism increasingly integrated its economic stakes with those of the Mexican bourgeoisie and state, a very clear dividing line polarizing the classes emerged. On one side of the line stood the triad of imperialism/state/domestic and foreign bourgeoisies; on the other side were much of the lower-paid intermediate classes, and the masses of workers, peasants, and underpaid, underemployed or unemployed people. Indeed, the major gap in Mexico's social structure continued to be between rich and poor, with growing numbers of intermediate-class families in most decades falling on the poorer side of the divide, as was the case in 1910.[25]

CLIENTELISM AND POLITICAL CULTURE

Cárdenas had enough charisma, popularity, and political skill to lay solid social foundations for a more rapid industrialization and accumulation of capital on an extended scale after his departure from the presidency in 1940. With such "stability," the state was able to introduce "modernizing" measures that encouraged the growth of monopoly capital. These steps included state financing of economic infrastructure; a phasing out of unproductive haciendas; and a readjustment or modification of foreign capital's dominance, especially in the energy sector where the state offered petroleum, gas, and electricity at reduced prices for the operation of large enterprises. Even so, the Mexican bourgeoisie never achieved complete class hegemony, one reason being that foreign capital continued to dominate the economy, the other reason being the stubborn persistence of the social movements of *los de abajo*.[26]

In the years 1940–2000, México was transformed into a semi-industrialized, highly urbanized country, with an abundant reserve of inexpensive labor power. Yet an unbalanced class structure and uneven income distribution, together with the existing demand structure and the character of the bourgeoisie and state, resulted in production being concentrated in what Marx theorized as "Department II" goods (consumer goods), mainly for the nation's affluent minority, as opposed to "Department I" goods (capital and intermediate goods, the means of production).

For its part, foreign capital increasingly shifted its activities into heavy and intermediate industry (including technology sales), agribusiness, tourism, and the financial and export sectors of the economy, with the result that it came to play a preponderant role in the character of the nation's economic growth and the state's economic decisionmaking. As in the past, and as in other developing nations, foreign loans and the external debt became bargaining chips used by foreign capitalists and their emerging "transnational corporations" to take over the commanding heights of the economy.

Meanwhile, a capitalist state, authoritarian and ever more technocratic, imposed "political stability." An historical continuity remained at the state and ideological levels. That continuity was embodied in the state's practices of co-optation and repression, corporatism, presidentialism, and ideological populism, which helped make intelligible the apparent "political stability" of Mexico during the first decades after 1940.

Under the Mexican corporatist system, when it came to national and local elections, the official political party served as the administrative committee for the affairs of the mass organizations. Political actors were not so much individuals or members of organizations, but instead were the ruling political party and the mass organizations' leadership. Because the official party held a monopoly of power within the mass organizations, no other party, old or new, had any significant political effect, at least within the electoral system, unless "the rules of the game" were changed (as happened in the 1990s because of social protest movements for democracy).

The PRI's corporatist state used revolutionary rhetoric to co-opt a significant part of the population and repression to crush more recalcitrant social activists or leftists. Even though Mexican anarchists, socialists, communists, and other leftists had played a pivotal role in organizing peasants and workers since the final decades of the nineteenth century, the corporatist state and its party defined them as "subversive," thus keeping them in a continuous minority status. The PRI's state used a "revolutionary" ideology to institutionalize a counterrevolution. By invoking the figures of Hidalgo, Morelos, Juárez, Madero, Villa, Zapata, Carranza, Obregón, and Cárdenas, the state was always able to accuse its opponents of being unpatriotic or "against the nation."

After violently crushing the student pro-democracy demonstrations of 1968 under this demagogic rationale, accusing the rebellious students of being "agents" of "foreign subversion," the government decided to place the students' principal historical inspiration, Ricardo Flores Magón, in the pantheon of national heroes, in spite of the bourgeoisie's previous denunciations of Flores Magón's proletarian internationalism as "anti-Mexican." Meanwhile, the very state that was behind the assassinations of peasant leaders like Rubén Jaramillo erected busts of their heads in village plazas.

In practice, the corporatist model of the Mexican state strengthened the political culture of clientelism. In the countryside, the tradition of *caciquismo* served to reinforce peasant and Indian susceptibility to following state tutelage or being co-opted. Peasant organizations were easily co-opted once their leaders were, since they typically had a shortage of personnel able quickly to become effective leaders in a capitalist system. Because of the organizations' paternalistic structures, co-opted leaders could easily bring the membership with them.

Marked by populist rhetoric and paternalistic content, *caciquismo* had always been characterized by a universally recognized streak of violence, capable of being called on at any moment with the help of private armies or the national armed forces. *Caciquismo* applied control with armed terror, and legitimized control with disarming spectacle—such as inauguration of a new school, clinic, or road. *Caciquismo* was also linked to religious or cultural ceremonies. These customs were in turn economically beneficial to merchants and local *caciques*, as "folklore" became "business," not just in the traditional manner of squeezing funds out of the poor to provide for ceremonial rituals, but in the modern modes of national and international tourism.

In the first decades after Cárdenas's presidency, clientelism and *caciquismo* flourished under the corporatist model, with its system of bribes, rewards, violence, co-optation, and control. Clientelism served to distract attention from growing class stratification and the conflict this generated in rural areas. It functioned in the same way, more or less, in the cities and all of society, for many years. Together with *caciquismo*, it contributed to a distinctively "*a la mexicana*" political culture that has lasted until the present. Since the 1960s, a big part of class struggle in Mexico has been directed against the mediating processes of *caciquismo* and clientelism.

An era of relative political stability in Mexico lasted until 1968, when the gigantic street demonstrations by pro-democracy students began attracting the support of growing numbers of workers, peasants, and even state employees. The military's massacre of hundreds of demonstrators on October 2, 1968, in Mexico City's Plaza of Three Cultures, was the beginning of the end of political stability. It was obvious that the ruling class and its state preferred repression over the practice of co-optation.[27] A minority of analysts would say that political stability lasted until 1988, when the PRI's candidate, Carlos Salinas de Gortari, lost the presidential election but, by the slimmest of margins, was declared the winner by the PRI-dominated elections board.

In the years since 1968, it is clear that Mexican political culture has maintained its "depth structure." In any Mexican struggle for a true democracy and an economy of social solidarity or socialism, it continues to be very difficult to overcome the problems of clientelism and repression, above all when so many people are having to deal each day with personal economic difficulties in a context of rising numbers of assassinations, massacres, robberies, and other forms of crime and abuse.

In 2010, monopoly capitalism is still in command, now fattened by the profits of the narcotraffic and reassured by a powerful military. The nation has been mortgaged more than ever to foreigners. Mexico is as sharply divided between rich and poor as it had been in 1910. And once again a significant number of Mexicans, however insurmountable their problems might seem, are beginning to respond with indignation, rage, and acts of self-organization to the tremors of earthquakes, sudden economic change, the handing over of their country to foreigners and narcos, and the political corruption affecting their daily lives.

CHAPTER FOUR

Neoliberal Terrorism, Immiseration, Destruction of Families

> We must abandon the idea of installing an American citizen in the Mexican presidency, as that would only lead us, once again, to war. The solution requires more time: we must open the doors of our universities to young, ambitious Mexicans and make the effort to educate them in the American way of life, in our values, and in respect for the leadership of the United States. Mexico will need competent administrators and, over time, these young people will come to occupy important positions and will eventually take possession of the presidency itself. And without the United States having to spend a single cent or fire a single shot, they will do what we want, and do it better and more radically than we ourselves could have done.
>
> —ROBERT LANSING, former Secretary of State under Woodrow Wilson, 1924

As we have seen, Mexico has been a principal target of the capitalist economic system and its imperialisms for more than a century. We can further understand Mexico's situation by examining it in the context of neoliberalism and imperialism in other parts of the world, especially Latin America.[1]

Since the 1973 U.S.-sponsored military coup d'état against a democratically elected socialist president in Chile, the economic terrorism of neoliberalism has spread to all the Americas, forcing millions of people to emigrate to more prosperous nations. The intermediate classes, from well-educated professionals to the traditional petty bourgeoisie, have no economic security. The working classes receive frozen or lower wages and, thanks to neoliberalism's "flexibilization of labor," can no longer find jobs that last. Latin American peasants and U.S. "family farmers" lose their lands, unemployment grows, and hunger spreads across the continent, including the United States.

In Latin America, economic neoliberalism and FTAs (Free Trade Agreements) imposed by imperialism and its allies, in governments like Chile's since 1973 and Mexico's since 1982, have undermined the region's local industries, farms, and employment opportunities, as well as any credibility or legitimacy in the limited "bourgeois democracies" won by popular struggles against the brutal military dictatorships of 1964–1982.

The people of Latin America and the Caribbean have reacted by intensifying the class struggle. Their social movements have toppled neoliberal governments and led to the election of leftist or centrist presidents who implement at least a few modest programs in favor of the most oppressed. These movements, like those in Mexico, continue to protest imperialism's privatization of nature, disruption of normal life, and use of their nations' illegitimate foreign debts to blackmail their governments and pillage their wealth.

Despite its military might, U.S. imperialism is weak. The United States finds itself in an economic and political crisis almost without precedent. Its dollar is losing world hegemony, one more reason it launches wars without end that it mistakenly assumes it can win in weak nations like Afghanistan and Iraq. The cost in U.S. lives has generated an antiwar movement by families of the dead and wounded. The economic expenses of military expansion have damaged the U.S. economy. Many generals have publicly expressed concern that their forces are too overextended to successfully resist the counterattacks of the peoples.

Meanwhile, the alter-globalization movement has made more people aware that the emperor is naked under his glitzy new robe of globalization that claims to promote human rights and sustainable development. Nevertheless, in the years prior to its current crisis, neoliberal capitalism generated an historic victory of monopoly capital against the working classes and small and medium-size businesses. Only now, with the financial crisis of recent years, is neoliberal capitalism starting to fall apart, at an even higher cost for the working and intermediate classes.

Behind the crisis are three decades of a world economy marked by slowly growing production and much speculation, especially in the mature capitalist economies. Financial speculation, narco and sex trafficking, money laundering, and arms sales for regional wars have become the economic engines of recent times. Many economists believe the profits in sex to be greater than those of narcotics, because women, youth, and children, unlike a narcotic, can be sold more than once.

According to some analysts, the global expansion of financial speculation and the centralization of banks and insurance companies have created a new dominant bourgeois fraction of *rentiers* (people of independent means, coupon clippers in effect). But the industrial and commercial bourgeoisies continue to be strong forces and influential voices, practicing, with the cooperation of the *rentiers* and the financial bourgeoisie, a wage enslavement that shovels bloodstained profits into the giant maws of all the bourgeois fractions. On one issue the bourgeoisies seem to be united: the *ideology* of neoliberalism and market fundamentalism represented by FTAs, whatever the depths of the economic crisis shaking the world after 2007 might be.

In the case of Mexico, the new "modernizing technocrats," graduates of Harvard and Yale and fanatical neoliberals, have been declared the winners of all the presidential elections starting in 1982. As anticipated almost a century ago by former U.S. secretary of state Robert Lansing in the citation opening this chapter, these technocrats have been "Americanized" and have done Washington's bidding "better and more radically than we ourselves could have done."

The results of their neoliberal policies have been horrific. The Mexican economy has suffered a long period of "stabilizing stagnation," a play on words used by some analysts to compare neoliberalism's impact with that of the preceding period of "stabilizing development." Since the start of neoliberal policies in 1982, the GNP (gross national product) has plummeted periodically—as much as 10 percent in 1994—putting an end to the absurd mantra of a "Mexican economic miracle."

According to the International Monetary Fund (IMF) and the World Bank, in 2009 the GNP fell 7 percent and the average income of workers lost 20 percent of its buying power. The Mexican government reported that the number of poor increased by 5 million. Today 51.3 percent of Mexico's population—estimated at 112 million—live in poverty, with another 25 percent in extreme poverty, and scarcely 20 percent remain securely above the poverty line. An estimated .07 percent possesses almost 40 percent of the national wealth.

In the first year of the Calderón government the cost of a *canasta básica*, that is, a basket of indispensable food for a family's health, increased 35 percent, and it is still rising. In March 2010, Mexico ranked fourth highest in inflation among the thirty nations that make up the Organization for Cooperation and Economic Development (OCDE). New taxes and increases in existing ones, including a sales tax hike to 16 percent, further worsened the economic situation of the intermediate and working classes, while the upper classes continued to benefit from the Mexican tradition of paying almost no taxes on their income.

According to Oxfam International, the Mexican countryside has suffered "devastation." A constitutional amendment in 1992 ended the *ejido* system, the only protection that peasants historically possessed in the face of the postSecond World War assault by giant domestic and foreign agribusinesses. Right away the percentage of rural proletarians shot up dramatically, from 46.2 percent in 1990 to 55.6 percent in 1995, and the class struggle in the countryside intensified. Soldiers, police, and paramilitaries of the political parties and agro-industry helped large-scale private interests dispossess the peasantry of its best land parcels. Indigenous and mestizo communities defending their lands were forcibly displaced and sometimes massacred, especially in the central and southern states. Among the bloodiest acts of repression were those in Aguas Blancas, Guerrero, in 1995; "the commune of Oaxaca," Lázaro Cárdenas, Michoacán, and San Salvador Atenco, Estado México, all in 2006; and Acteal, Chiapas, in 1997. These are only the tip of the iceberg.

Now some twenty transnational corporations in food, fertilizers, and agriculture control the nation's farming and livestock sector, largely for export. Thanks to NAFTA, Mexico has lost its relative self-sufficiency in food production. NAFTA has generated in Mexico duty-free sales of corn and other products of transnational corporations subsidized by the U.S. government, like Cargill, Monsanto, DuPont-Pioneer, and Dow, at prices lower than those of local products. Consequently, the prices of the harvests of the peasantry have plummeted 70 percent.

According to a Carnegie Endowment report, in the first decade of NAFTA, 1.8 million peasants had to abandon their lands. Unable to compete and lacking credits and other necessary resources, the peasants headed for Mexico's cities or the United States, leaving behind mostly women and children who have not been able to produce more than the minimum for their own consumption. Agrarian analyst Armando Bartra speaks of the "feminization of the countryside." New organizations like the Consejo Nacional de Campesinos (CONOC) demand that the government reorient its agrarian policies and take action against the monopolies.

The transnational corporations' sales of transgenic seeds continue the destruction of more traditional forms of production in harmony with *Madre Tierra* (Mother Nature). This represents a form of bioterrorism against the peasants who cannot compete with imported products or defend against transgenic displacement of native varieties such as the several types of Mexican corn.[2]

Millions of rag-clad Mexicans wander across the volcanic landscape of mountainous escarpments, eroded hillsides, drought-plagued valleys, arid deserts, and overcrowded cities, following the harvest trail or searching for a day's work. About 4 million are street venders in the teeming capital, Mexico City, veiled in fumes spewed by industrial smokestacks and automobiles stuck in traffic jams. Less than half the workforce is regularly employed, and only a fourth of them earn the minimum wage, which is sufficient for less than half of what a family of five needs to maintain itself. Half the peasantry goes to bed hungry. The bottom half of the population, including 90 percent of preschool children, suffers from malnutrition and goes barefoot. They have no plumbing, no safe drinking water, and no electricity.

"Today is like yesterday," sighs a popular Mexican song, "in a world without tomorrow. How sad the rain beats on the tin roofs of the cardboard houses."

But can't Mexico improve the lives of its citizens with the money generated by the petroleum and gas industry? No, not unless there's a new nationalization to reverse the impact of the years of privatization. More than half of the production of the state oil firm PEMEX goes to the United States. Mexico is the only nation with a special petroleum deal with the United States: it guarantees supplying the U.S. Strategic Oil Reserve at low cost.

Because of this deal and huge U.S. loans and technology sales to develop the oil and gas industry, as well as thousands of concessions to about two dozen transnational corporations in the natural gas and petrochemical sectors and for new explorations, Mexico no longer securely controls the fate of its own hydrocarbon resources. Nor does it control its other natural resources, including the labor power that emigrates to the United States.

Oil prices soared for many years, so where did all the PEMEX income go and where does it go now? It paid and pays the transnationals for their investments: the banks for the interest on the internal and external Mexican debt; its own debt; and other expenses—not to mention the traditional robbery and graft on the part of state officials and union leaders.

According to "Mexico 2030, Proyecto de Gran Visión,"[3] between the years 2009 and 2018 contracts of the parastate enterprise Federal Commission of Electricity will allot billions of dollars to a public-private association, another form of privatization. *Fortune* magazine, the newspaper *El Financiero*, and other business bibles have concluded that market forces will lead to the complete denationalization of Mexico's energy sector, perhaps by modifying the Constitution as was done in 1992 to privatize the *ejidos*.

In truth, all the principal facts about "neoliberal globalization" and "free trade" boil down to one word: imperialism. U.S. leaders themselves have said as much. The highest U.S. trade representative once proclaimed, "Globalization is the United States." President Bill Clinton told an AFL-CIO convention that free trade "is about how 4 percent of the world's people can continue to hold 22 percent of the world's wealth." One of President George W. Bush's secretaries of state publicly declared about NAFTA: "Our goal is to guarantee that national companies control a territory that extends from the Arctic to Antarctica and free access without any kind of obstacle."

In other words, contemporary imperialism is globalization, and FTAs help the empire annex Latin America. All the "plans"

(Plan Mexico, Plan Colombia, etc.), although advertised as "economic integration and sustainable development," are, in fact, the military wing of FTAs, a form of recolonization of Latin America. It all adds up to the desperate and predatory quest for lucre that has always characterized colonial and imperialist systems. Without capital accumulation on an extended scale, in other words ever more profits, capitalism simply cannot survive.[4]

IMMISERATION

It's the same with "sustainable development," a concept introduced by ecologists and fervently adopted by the World Bank and other institutions of the empire to cover up the criminal destruction of the environment and indigenous communities by their mega-dams and other large-scale projects on behalf of transnational corporations. Sustainable development has not slowed the rhythm of the peasants' loss of lands or the underpayment of rural and urban workers, but, on the contrary, it has helped *sustain* it. In addition, it has led to increased access to peasant knowledge about local flora and fauna to the benefit of the transnationals, especially the timber, agricultural, and pharmaceutical interests. Monsanto and a handful of drug manufacturers are taking advantage of the "intellectual property rights related to commerce" recognized by the World Trade Organization (WTO) to plunder the world's flora and fauna—a "biopiracy" that includes the pillage of the specialized knowledge of the original peoples, a 500-year colonial tradition in Latin America that led to the medical "discoveries" underlying much of today's "modern" medicine.

Mexico is one of the biggest customers of the World Bank. It continues receiving huge World Bank loans that supposedly create projects "targeting poverty" but instead perpetuate it—"sustainable underdevelopment," as it were. One of these World Bank projects was the sadly celebrated strategy of "investment in the poor" implemented in the 1970s and 1980s. It aimed to keep peasants producing on their small parcels of land as supervised unfree labor and to obtain their surplus food and handicraft production through the control of the market for distribution, the sale of seeds, fertilizers, insecticides, and machinery, and the provision of credit. It also aimed to "help" poor women and men in the cities with credits to incorporate *them* into the "free market."

The first full-scale "investment in the poor" pilot project commercialized a remote area in the states of Oaxaca, Puebla, and Veracruz by harnessing the energy of the Papaloapán River and the labor of 1.5 million members of hillside peasant families. The peasants produced immense quantities of cheap foodstuffs but were left worse off—having to increase their subsistence farming just to sustain themselves. The "investment in the poor" strategy perpetuated poverty because—in German sociologist Veronika Bennholdt-Thomsen's words—"it is not the lack of market integration, rather its increase, which leads to the immiseration of the peasants."[5]

The point here is that the immiseration of the majority of Mexicans serves the interests of the transnationals and their accumulation of capital. Although not counted in the statistics of the "economically active population," dozens of millions of Mexicans work for a pittance as subcontracted seamstresses (and others involved in "industrial homework"), shepherds, carpenters, artisans, street vendors, carriers, messengers, household servants, laundresses, shoe-shiners, car washers, car watchers, marketplace stall operators, lottery ticket sellers, irregularly employed factory hands, small-scale workshop employees or owners, and so forth. Untold numbers slave as "owners" of *misceláneas*—corner shops that sell soft drinks, cookies, cigarettes, and similar items.

While technically unemployed or underemployed, most are in fact "overemployed," often working more than one job per person and at least two jobs per adult couple per family, without counting the millions of children who work long hours. Women take on more and more paid and unpaid work, while children and the aged work when and where they can.

The number of overemployed and superexploited[6] has grown with the economic collapse of hundreds of thousands of small and medium industries during NAFTA's reign and the recent economic crisis. Every year a growing number of wage workers rotate in and out of the ranks of the technically unemployed and underemployed, reducing the differences separating unionized from nonunionized workers. A subcontracting system of temp workers in heavy and light industries is now the common rule in neoliberal Mexico.

In all their "jobs," the immiserated help the economy, directly and indirectly, including their selling the goods of the transnationals on the street or in their *misceláneas*. They contribute to the capitalists' extraction of surplus value by helping to meet the costs of the production of labor power on a daily basis and to maintain the labor force.[7] The various jobs undertaken by the immiserated further integrate them with capital's accumulation process, either through their direct production of surplus value or through their role in the circulation, distribution, and servicing of commodities and their own consumption of goods.

A good example of their production of surplus value is their widespread operation of hundreds of thousands of sweatshops, or "domestic workshops," especially in industries like clothing and footwear. Since the number of these in various industries has risen in the neoliberal era—in part because of the working classes' feverish attempts to compensate for their inadequate earnings or employment—they cannot be viewed as precapitalist modes of production destined to disappear.

On the contrary, these workshops are a product and tool of modern capitalist accumulation and form an important part of the much-ballyhooed "new international division of labor." They have nothing to do with "marginalization" and everything to do with "integration" of the immiserated into contemporary capitalism. It is for these reasons, and not humanitarian ones, that the World Bank decided as early as 1977 to invest more in the *misceláneas* and various other economic activities of the urban poor.[8]

Karl Marx characterized a *relative surplus population* as a "condition of existence of the capitalist mode of production." He pointed out that industrial capitalism "depends on the constant formation, the greater or less absorption, and the reformation of the industrial reserve army or surplus population, independently of the absolute growth of the population."[9] In this sense, the roots of immiseration of millions of Mexicans have had little to do with population growth (which, in fact, has been slowing down since 1970) and everything to do with the nature of capitalist production and its penetration into the remotest areas of the countryside and urban slums.

To the extent that monopoly capital and its productive processes transcend national borders, turning into transnationals, the labor force also becomes more mobile and starts to cross borders—but at a much slower rate than capital. For the monopoly capitalists based in the more industrialized countries, this permits easy access to a growing reserve army of workers and an even higher rate of profit. In the long run it has a negative impact on unionized workers and their salaries in the industrialized countries. In fact, they are already experiencing a process of "informalization" of the formal sectors of the economy, such as in the U.S. electronics and automotive spare parts industries.

The immiserated are simultaneously necessary for the capitalist productive process and a critical force in the struggle to replace it with a more democratic, collective, or socialist one. This was dramatically illustrated in 1985 when an earthquake devastated Mexico City. Women seamstresses and "their" sewing machines were buried in the rubble when the absentee capitalists sent trucks not to rescue the women but to take away the sewing machines. Soldiers stood guard to prevent the women's relatives and friends from interfering with the rescue of the machines. Within days, seamstresses walking on crutches led a protest march of thousands. They demanded, and soon obtained, the right to unionize, placing them and their new union in the front ranks of what soon became a mass movement for democracy in Mexico.

It's not for nothing that the imperialists have invested millions of dollars in aid projects for the poor and in the weaponry to control them. U.S. arms sales for the Mexican state's repressive apparatuses have included highly sophisticated military technology for special shock forces and elite SWAT teams assigned to controlling the multitudes, for counterinsurgency warfare, and in general for the maintenance of internal stability or "governability." In spite of neoliberalism's pretensions of eliminating state intervention to leave everything to the magical workings of the free market, the role of the state remains essential not only for privatizations but for repression, the militarization of society, and the co-optation, bureaucratization, and technocratic organization of protesting social groups, always with the "humanitarian" help of nongovernmental organizations (NGOs) loyal to their funding sources in the wealthiest nations. All these trends are evident in Mexico.

Such control over the immiserated masses has been succeeding. Most of the "daily life" organizational networks of the immiserated are not politically progressive: petty crime syndicates; male-dominated family systems; overdependence on religious or social institutions like the *compadrazgo* (which does have a positive side in economic survival terms); traditional deference to *el patrón* and related informal patron-client systems; and so on. At the same time, the immiserated have participated in growing numbers in the social movements that have erupted since the 1985 earthquake. Critical to that process have been the struggles by women and the original peoples against oppression and for the preservation of their families and communities.

DESTRUCTION OF FAMILIES: THE ORIGINAL PEOPLES AND WOMEN RISE UP, THE RIGHT AND THE CHURCH COUNTERATTACK

Since the neo-Zapatista uprising of 1994 in the southern state of Chiapas and even before it, the original peoples and women have been filling the front ranks of all Mexico's social movements for political and economic change. In part this is because neoliberalism has destroyed so many families. Women in particular have responded to this with righteous anger and considerable courage.

"Comandanta Esther" of the Ejército Zapatista de Liberación Nacional (EZLN) put it well in a speech on International Women's Day, March 8, 2001:

> Once grown up I began to see that we didn't have adequate food, that others did and we didn't. Why didn't we? I saw that I had four or five little brothers and sisters who had died, that's when I realized: "Why were my little brothers and sisters dying?" I saw that it was necessary to fight, because if I didn't do anything other brothers and sisters would keep on dying, and I decided. And not only me, there are women who decided to be soldiers, and those women now have the insurgent rank of Captain, of Major, of Lieutenant. So there we see that yes women can. . . . To women throughout the country, we are saying, let us fight together. We have to fight more, because as indigenous we are triply looked down upon: as indigenous women, as women, and as poor women. But women who are not indigenous also suffer. That is why we are inviting all of them to fight, so that we will not continue to suffer. It's not true that women don't know, that they're not good at anything except being in the home. That doesn't happen only in the indigenous communities but also in the cities.[10]

Here we must look at how neoliberalism and the state impact on the family in today's world. Mexico's capitalist neoliberal state delivers far fewer social services than the capitalist welfare state of Cárdenas did in the 1930s or the PRI's dictatorial and clientelist state did between 1941 and 1982. The neoliberal state is each day more privatized and a repressive apparatus for the national and international bourgeoisies. In spite of its religious and ethical rhetoric, it has little genuine interest in the well-being of the families of the masses. The family is normally the source of whatever collective solidarity and responsibility people feel in their daily lives, in part owing to the decline of the trade unions, churches, and other traditional sources of social collective responsibility.

As neoliberalism leads to a growing destruction of families, however, other networks of daily participation and collective solidarity gain importance, especially among women and youth. The alternative networks are quite diverse and include various subcultures: neighborhood gangs, communal dining halls, narcotics networks, community cooperatives, Christian base communities, independent media, and music, dance, muralist, ecology, sports, sexual preference, new age, and media networks. When people have less economic hope for the future they usually seek individualistic solutions, but when those fail they start looking at alternatives such as social movements and other popular struggles that provide a palpable sense of solidarity and collective responsibility.[11]

In Mexico, the original peoples and women remain central to any successful political transformation. Census data show that there are ten million indigenous that speak sixty languages with 364 linguistic variants. Close to a third of the Mexican population is predominantly Indian, although many of them share the culture of the more than 60 percent who are mestizos. Ethnicity, like race, continues to be a *social construction* related to one's class and social position in society, what anthropologists and ethnographers call "situational identities."

Over 76 percent of Mexico's original peoples live in *extreme poverty*. The diverse indigenous peoples (Mayans, Mixtecs, Purépechas, Zapotecs, and many others), or what anthropologist

Guillermo Bonfil Batalla calls "Deep Mexico,"[12] are committed as much to a class struggle within the capitalist economy as to a cultural battle against society's racism and for the preservation of their traditions. For them, land is not a commodity to be bought and sold but an integral part of their worldview of respect for nature, for "Madre Tierra" (their Virgin of Guadalupe). Their demand for "autonomy" signifies not only local self-governance in accord with their traditions of collective decision-making but also control over the lands, rivers, and other elements of nature they have long respected and understood in ways that run counter to capitalism's aggressive exploitation of these resources.

The CIA has frequently characterized the social movements of the original peoples as a major challenge to U.S. hegemony. Territories they occupy contain 80 percent of Latin America's biodiversity, several important watersheds, and such valuable resources as oil, precisely the situation that exists in Chiapas. Convention 169 of the International Labor Organization (ILO) and the UN's Declaration of Rights of Indigenous Peoples recognize the territorial and cultural rights of the original peoples.[13]

The original peoples' cultures harmonize particularly well with the class struggle since land is the only means of survival for so many rural people in superexploitative situations like those created by neoliberalism. The land question was the main reason the neo-Zapatistas launched their armed revolt in 1994, as reflected in their Magonista slogan of "*Tierra y Libertad*" and their many proclamations. At the same time, the Zapatistas' fight against "globalized" capitalism led them to emphasize internationalism, above all in defense of an alter-globalization based on the values of Latin America's original peoples, the values of collective solidarity and respect for human and planetary rights, including the rights of nature—"Madre Tierra" (or in South America "*Pachamama*," literally "Mother Universe").

Since 1994, the neo-Zapatista influence has spread from Chiapas to almost all of the indigenous communities of Mexico (and other parts of the world, including Venezuela). The Zapatistas have created autonomous municipalities and *Juntas de Buen Gobierno* (JBG) (Juntas of Good Government) that act outside the political system of the rest of the country. The JBG incorporate all the communities, which periodically meet in general assemblies. They program the participation of women and youth and give them central roles, reflecting a direct, participatory democracy. Frequent rotation of leaders is mandatory—it is not just the right of recall, or revoking a leader's position if he fails to fulfill the custom of *mandar obedeciendo* (to lead by obeying). No military leader of the EZLN and no member of the Comité Clandestino Revolucionario Indígena (CCRI)—the collective "command" of the EZLN—can occupy a post of authority in the autonomous municipalities. The EZLN's job is to protect the citizenry from the soldiers of the Mexican army.[14]

Traditions of co-optation, *caciquismo*, and violent repression by the state continue to divide the original peoples. Nevertheless, the overwhelming majority of them reject the state policy known as *indigenismo*, a form of assimilation that has perpetuated "ethnocide and negation of the citizen and collective rights of their villages and communities."[15] That is why the influential Congreso Nacional Indígena (CNI), founded in 1996 and independent of the EZLN although in favor of its program, emphatically rejected Congress's 2001 "reform," which both broke the San Andrés Accords reached by the government and Zapatista negotiators during peace talks and maintained the features of *indigenismo*.

The situation in Chiapas has become increasingly precarious since then, because of a "dirty war" type of militarization, paramilitarization, and payment of select Indian groups to attack others. The Zapatistas and many indigenous communities in the rest of Mexico continue pursuing their self-organization of autonomy while pacifically resisting the new wave of killings, massacres, disappearances, and incarcerations. They are a national political force fighting for a new constituent assembly to draft a new constitution. Anthropologist Gilberto López y Rivas has concluded that the key part of the Zapatista program is "indigenous autonomy" that incorporates "egalitarian, participatory, self-generated and collectivist principles . . . to successfully confront capitalism, preserve the human species from self-destruction, and democratize our societies."[16]

In all the social movements and not just the rising up of the original peoples, women have been participating in an outstanding way, at times with an element of surprise. An example is the "Adelitas"—brigades of women so named after the *soldaderas* (women soldiers) who fought in Pancho Villa's "Division of the North" during the Revolution. For two months in 2006 the Adelitas were the main force of the huge and historical sit-in (*plantón*) along the Paseo de la Reforma and side streets near Mexico City's huge downtown plaza, the Zócalo, in demand of a vote recount and recognition of the electoral victory of "*el Presidente legítimo*," López Obrador. In the spring of 2008 they seized the Senate and paralyzed it to prevent the attempt by the PRI and PAN to privatize petroleum by secret ballot. They were accompanied by their male counterparts, the "*Adelitos*." Some 50,000 people in more than forty brigades of *Adelitas y Adelitos* have organized themselves in cities and towns across the land to continue defending the best values of Mexico with their creative and militant tactics.

According to government statistics, 51.6 percent of the Mexican population is female; 25 percent of households are headed by women. Mexico's labor force is 40 percent female, but only half of them work in the "formal sector" of the economy and, on average, they earn 37 percent less than males doing similar tasks. Women get few jobs in sectors paying good salaries. Thirty percent of them say they suffer violence at their workplaces; 19 percent say they suffer violence in their homes. Because of that, many of them live alone or with other women. In addition, for economic survival reasons, it has become a custom for women to head households where more than a single family resides.

Almost all women do their own housework in their homes, that is, many women work "the double day"—in reality "the triple day" if one takes into account all the activities of women in the *generational production of labor power*.[17] Production of labor power *does not have to be feminized or unwaged.* It is the patriarchy and machismo that socially structures, maintains, and exaggerates the superexploitation of women. That is why the struggle for improvement of the working class as a whole must take up the struggles for women's equal rights and the socialization of labor power production. A class analysis without a gendered analysis does not reflect the "real world."[18]

Of Mexico's female population over fourteen years of age, 62 percent work without pay, mainly in other people's households or in their own homes. Thus, women subsidize capitalism through their unpaid labor in "domestic economies" as well as in their underpaid work in capitalist enterprises—and they have been essential to both, including the transnational corporations that have set up *maquiladoras* (low-wage high-tech assembly plants) all over Mexico. Women's unpaid domestic work facilitates employers' ability to pay all workers lower wages, while related patriarchic ideologies and gendered practices make women even more superexploitable.

Statistical estimates by the United Nations and other institutions indicate that women provide two-thirds of the world's recorded hours of work but obtain only one-tenth of the world's income and possess less than a hundredth of its wealth. Of a global population of more than 6 billion people, 4.5 billion earn less than two dollars a day—70 percent of those superexploited individuals are women and children.

Labor historian and trade unionist Dan La Botz has pointed out the critical role of women in the attempted resurgence by trade unionism so weakened by neoliberalism:

> All Mexican workers, and all workers in Canada and the United States—for we are now all part of the same labor movement—owe a

> debt of gratitude to the Mexican women. Had there been no women's movement, there could have been no new labor reform movement. The rising of the women has also been the rising of the working class, has been the rising of us all.[19]

Emblematic of women's labor militancy today is the Frente Nacional de Mujeres en Lucha por la Dignidad de Trabajadores (National Front of Women in Struggle for Workers' Dignity) founded during a national assembly of the Union of Miners. As everyone knows, it is almost impossible to organize an independent union like the Union of Miners. There is too much repression, *charrismo*, corruption, and bureaucracy. Also, there are the anti-labor decisions of the government, the Federal Board of Conciliation and Arbitration, and the courts of a state marked by "failed law."

Héctor de la Cueva, director of the NGO Centro de Investigación Laboral y Asesoría Sindical (Center of Labor Research and Trade Union Consultancy), has written that "the Mexican working class and trade unionism are in one of the worst situations that they have lived in in recent decades." This was also the conclusion of the International Tribunal of Trade Union Freedom summarized in this book's opening chapters. Even so, through their struggles Mexico's workers have managed to create independent unions with women leading the fight for honest trade unionism and other good causes, starting with the founding of the Authentic Labor Front (FAT) fifty years ago.[20]

The Coordinadora Nacional de Trabajadores de Educación (CNTE, National Coordinating Committee of Education Workers), a breakaway union of schoolteachers, received many women leaders tired of their second-class status in the corrupt Sindicato Nacional de Trabajadores de Educación (SNTE, National Union of Education Workers), even though 70 percent of its 1.4 million members are female. The current "*jefe máxima*" (first chief) of this *charro* union is Elba Esther Gordillo Morales, who opportunistically broke with the PRI to support the PAN where she could make more money. She has backed the proposed reform known as the Alianza para la Calidad de la Educación (ACE) (Alliance for Quality Education). The CNTE says ACE will privatize education and create worse conditions for the already underpaid and overworked schoolteachers.

Many bilingual indigenous women are CNTE leaders. They have played an important role in the social movements of the poorest states, including "the commune of Oaxaca."[21] The Coalition for Justice in the Maquiladoras (CJM), founded in 1989,[22] is a tri-national workers' coalition based in San Antonio, Texas, that has female leadership. In 2010 it presented a formal complaint to the ILO documenting a long history in the *maquiladoras* of violations of the ILO's Conventions 87 and 98 on trade union autonomy, the right to organize, and the right to collective bargaining. In Mexico, 90 percent of union contracts—and even more in the *maquila* sector—are "protection contracts," arranged by the employers with *charro* union leaders whom they have selected with the cooperation of the Mexican government. During a forum celebrating its twentieth anniversary, the CJM proclaimed its militant program, which incorporated gender equality, freedom of sexual preference, and solidarity with other social movements, workers' rights, and revolutionary processes in the Americas.

Women constitute 11 percent of the Sindicato Mexicano de Electricistas (SME), whose members were illegally dismissed from a hundred electric power plants by 5,000 PFP police, 10,000 police reserves, and 3,000 military officers on October 10, 2009. Ninety percent of the SME's female members are heads of family and 10 percent joined the massive hunger strike in the Zócalo launched by SME militants seeking justice in April 2010. Dozens of women and men in other cities participated in rotating hunger strikes to support the electrical workers. Women from the families of the dismissed SME workers set up food stands and a permanent garage sale to support the approximately 18,000 SME workers who refused the untrustworthy economic packages offered by the government in exchange for accepting their unemployment and the busting of their union.

By April 2010, the impressive mobilizations of the SME, the miners, and other independent unions forced the *charros*' main union confederations to come out against the PAN's ultra right-wing labor reform: the Confederación de Trabajadores de Mexico (CTM), the Congreso del Trabajo (CT), the Confederación Regional Obrero Mexicana (CROM), and the Confederación Revolucionaria de Obreros and Campesinos (COR). The CTM and CT said they would back the proposal of the PRI, gearing up for the July elections. The Unión Nacional de Trabajadores (UNT), a coalition of unions that had left the CT in order to combat *charrismo*, had internal divisions. The UNT's telephone workers supported the "lite" proposal for labor reform offered by the Partido de la Revolución Democrática (PRD), because it had fewer negative consequences for workers. The UNT's university unions, the SME, the Sindicato de Mineros, and the CNTE, on the other hand, had more revolutionary visions and maintained their position against any of the labor reform proposals.[23]

Feminicide in Mexico has also contributed to the destruction of families and strongly influenced the rising up of women. The CJM organized against feminicide from the outset, while in 2009 the Inter-American Court of Human Rights found against the Mexican state on the same crime and also decided to consider the case of the forced disappearance of a Mexican woman.

As the internationalist feminist Josefina Chávez Rodríguez has noted, the anti-drug war declared by Calderón "is sowing the power of fear." In a prominent journal she helped found, she writes:

> Today women are assassinated in all of the Mexican Republic for the mere fact of being a woman, and that phenomenon exists in

> other countries—violence against women, in wild capitalism. . . . Today, thousands of individuals and families have lost one or more members of their family; there is a state of shock.[24]

The rising of the women has played a strong role in the campaign for the right to free and safe abortion. In April 2007, more than thirty years after the second wave of the feminist movement in Mexico began its fight for that right and ten years after the PRD began governing the Federal District (DF) (greater Mexico City), the DF's Legislative Assembly depenalized abortion up to the twelfth week of gestation, with no restriction whatsoever and with access to public health services.

The right wing didn't take long to respond. In May 2007, the head of the National Commission of Human Rights and the nation's attorney general presented legal briefs questioning the constitutionality of that historic legislation. Nevertheless, a year later, in August 2008, after public hearings without precedent, the Suprema Corte de Justicia de la Nación (SCJN) (Supreme Court) declared it constitutional.[25]

So, two months later, the right wing tried another tactic. The PAN and the PRI launched a national offensive at the legislative level to surround the DF with "pro-life" states, promoting the introduction into state constitutions of "the right to life from the moment of conception." By May 2010, the right had achieved this type of constitutional reform in eighteen states. In some of them it changed penal and health codes to explicitly criminalize women who voluntarily interrupt their pregnancies. In some instances, these legislative changes were supported by the local congressional representatives of all the leftist parties.

It didn't take long for women in the social movements and their supporters to respond. In all of the states involved, they conducted press conferences, street actions, legal defense of jailed women, and other protests. But there was usually a lack of coordinated efforts with other states. One exception was the formation of an interstate coordinating committee between groups in Guanajuato, Michoacán, and Veracruz. Meanwhile, NGOs in the DF with long experience of the issue continued their efforts at a national level. Internationally, a few congresswomen attended a meeting of the Second International to argue that the position taken by the PRI in favor of the states' "right to life" constitutional reforms was incompatible with its permanent attendance there, an argument that received the endorsement of several of the most prominent leaders of the Second International.

In mid-2009, when the right-wing offensive was rolling along in high gear, Feministas Socialistas (FS) [Socialist Feminists], based in the DF, began planning a national forum to unite the efforts of the women working in the states and then to link them with the NGOs and other organizations headquartered in the capital to facilitate a response with stronger punch. For months, FS sought funding for the forum, usually via the NGOs, but the quest proved fruitless. Not a single foundation or NGO offered a penny for that kind of activity.

In spite of this, on December 5, 2009, with support only from the personal financing offered by two women legislators, various groups and individuals from eighteen parts of the country, including the traditional DF groups, convened the National Forum on the Right to Decide. About 170 women from thirty-five organizations in nineteen states and from fifty-five organizations in the DF attended, along with several women who participated on their own account. They drafted and signed the "Pact for Life, Liberty, and Women's Rights" platform that called for:

- Defense of the right to decide and freedom for women criminalized for exercising their right to abort;
- Defense of the laical state and opposition to interventions by any church trying to impose its values upon the citizenry as a whole;

- Public denunciation of female and male politicians who voted in favor of the aforementioned local reforms of state constitutions;
- Fight for the right to health and the depenalization of abortion throughout the country.

They also agreed to conduct nationwide activities to defend this platform on the first Thursday of each month.

The constant pressures began to stall the right-wing offensive. For example, the PRI had to retreat in Veracruz, where the legislature in its second round of voting did not approve its own law on the rights of the fetus, and the PRI state governor had to promise pardons for women incarcerated for having had an abortion. By the end of May 2010, he had not fulfilled his promise, and there are indigenous women in his state condemned to eighteen years in prison convicted of homicide for having had an abortion. But the simple fact that he had to make the promise is a result of the citizenry's political pressure.

In May 2010, the Supreme Court ruled that use of the emergency pill is constitutional. The SCJN also accepted for review the case of 100 women imprisoned in Puebla for having had an abortion. A month earlier, legislators and functionaries of the PRD and other centrist and left-of-center political parties organized themselves into a "Network of Politicians Working for the Rights and the Non-criminalization of Women in Mexico." This was important in light of the fact that for eighteen months congress members claiming to be leftists had joined the PAN/PRI offensive against a woman's right to decide about her body.

In Mexico, as in the rest of the world, the rights of lesbian, gay, bisexual, and transgender people (LGBT) are violated every day. But in the greater area of Mexico City there are annual marches of thousands of persons in defense of LGBT rights. Moreover, in March 2010 a new law recognizing same-sex marriage and permitting same-sex couples to adopt took effect in the DF, an historic first in Latin America and the Caribbean.

Despite these examples of success, by no means is the war over. The PAN, on principle, continues its offensive, allied with the Catholic Church, which continues its public campaign in defense of the patriarchy and against charges, with evidence, of its own officials' sexual abuse. There's an initiative in Congress to reform the Constitution in order to protect "the right to life from the moment of conception." Also, there are appeals before the SCJN questioning the constitutionality of the new DF law permitting same-sex marriage.[26]

To understand the role of the Catholic Church, we must recall Mexican history. The 1917 Constitution was the most anticlerical in the Americas. It prohibited foreign priests from working in Mexico; the Church from possessing properties; religious schools, seminaries and convents; Catholic priests' right to vote; and any cleric's mention of politics in public. In the 1920s and 1930s, the government tried to enforce the Constitution. The persecution of the Church became ferocious, and by 1933 there remained only 300 priests in all Mexico—albeit underground, operating clandestinely. In 1938 the persecution ended but the Constitution still threatened the clergy.

The defeated Church kept a low profile until the early 1980s, but when the government swung toward the right and neoliberalism, the high clergy came out of the closet and began to opine on the questions of the day, taking conservative positions. After stealing the 1988 election, president-elect Carlos Salinas de Gortari struck a secret deal with the ecclesiastical authorities, and the bishops used their influence to get the infuriated masses to stop demonstrating against the electoral fraud. In 1992, President Salinas completed his part of the secret deal and removed the majority of the anticlerical articles from the Constitution. The Catholic hierarchy then started an offensive to penetrate Mexican politics.[27]

How does the high clergy conduct itself? Monsignor Norberto Rivera Carrera shut down the Seminary of the Southeast that taught the theology of liberation and warred against the ecclesiastical base communities that worked with the poor in the teeming slums of Netzahualcóyotl, Mexico City. Now Cardinal Rivera champions neoliberalism and accompanies the high and mighty to their fiestas. The cardinal has access to their private jets to visit the Vatican. Sociological studies show that the richest social strata are almost as religious as the poorest (for opposite reasons).[28]

In 1983, Monsignor Juan Posadas Ocampo arrived in Cuernavaca to repress the progressive church of retired Bishop Sergio Méndez Arceo and the 800 ecclesiastical base communities in Morelos. He did his work so well that the Vatican promoted him to cardinal and sent him to Guadalajara. The cardinal enjoyed a luxurious mansion and a Gran Marquis Blanco car, with chauffeur, given to him by millionaires of the automotive industry and other generous upper-class folk. This is the kind of car the Mafia drives. In 1993 when the cardinal drove to the airport to receive the papal nuncio Jerónimo Prigione, gunmen of two rival cartels were having a shootout. One of the men from the cartel of Joaquín Guzmán Loera, a.k.a "El Chapo" (Shorty), saw the Gran Marquis Blanco and pumped fourteen bullets into the heart of the cardinal.[29]

There are photographs of the Vatican's secretary, Angelo Sodano, in Chile on a platform with state terrorist Augusto Pinochet. Sodano, the "grey eminence" behind Pope John Paul II, assigned reactionary bishops to Mexico from 1990 on. About the exasperating situation of the Church, Javier Sicilia, a devout Catholic and one of the most outstanding intellectuals of Mexico, recently pronounced: "It's obvious that in its condition of being a social thing, an institution, the Church is—as pointed out by a part of the ancient formula that defines it—a *meretriz*, a whore."[30]

Sicilia is referring to the institution and not to Jesuits who work for human rights and sometimes have sacrificed their lives in defense of the people. He is not referring to Dominicans like Monsignor Raúl Vera López who has worked with the original peoples, or to the Franciscans who are disciples of Christ. He is not talking about the parish priests who work with the poor. He is criticizing the princes of the Church like Cardinal Norberto Rivera; people have asked the courts of Los Angeles to mandate his extradition so that he might be tried for protecting pederasts.

There is a darker side to the religious right and its social influence. Many of the superrich are disciples of Opus Dei, the Legionnaires of Christ,[31] and the Yunque, a secret Mexican society that admires the deceased Spanish dictator Francisco Franco and works to establish a fascist government in Mexico. Its goal is to make the government follow the dictates of the Catholic Church; so it infiltrates its members into the highest spheres of political power. According to Álvaro Delgado, an investigative reporter for the weekly *Proceso*, various top businessmen and many politicians of the PAN are members of the Yunque. Delgado affirms that PAN leaders like César Nava Vazquez are *yunquistas* who control the party's structure.[32]

The *yunquistas* are in many branches of government. They include Luis Felipe Bravo Mena, secretary of de facto president Calderón, the influential advertising executive Luis Pazos, and the former president of PAN and a possible PAN candidate for the 2012 presidential election, Manuel Espino Barrientos, although he denies it. The businessman Carlos Abascal Carranza, labor secretary of President Fox (2000–2006), notorious for his public condemnations of independent women and honest labor leaders, was a *yunquista*. He died of cancer in 2008, and now the Mexican right wants to beatify the deceased and declare him a saint.

There is a real danger of a social explosion in today's Mexico, as all observers, including the Catholic Church, recognize and fear. For that reason, and to protect its image as a supposed force for peace, the Church, like so many other Mexicans, has called for the return of the army to its barracks—because so many "violations of human rights are happening."[33] In light of the deepening economic crisis, the rising level of human rights violations, and the dangers involved, a brief analysis of the latest national and international events in the areas of migration, human and nature's rights, politicking, and popular mobilizations of resistance becomes absolutely necessary.

CHAPTER FIVE

Migration, Human and Nature's Rights, Politicking, Resistance

> There exists a fake, false republic. . . a group has confiscated all the powers . . . around 30 [persons] make up the central committee of the Mexican oligarchy. . . . This species of Mafioso government or covert dictatorship not only has nullified democratic life but has brought about an infamous and immoral economic and social inequality . . . they are obsessed with continuing the sacking even if they destroy Mexico.
>
> —ANDRÉS MANUEL LÓPEZ OBRADOR[1]

The winds of dignified rage, and even hope without fear, are blowing from the "empire's harvest"—that is, from the immigrant peoples, mainly those from Mexico and the rest of Latin America, whose labor is so critically important for the sustenance of the U.S. economy. While NAFTA and other free-trade agreements continue to expel workers from the South because of the collapse of local agriculture and manufacturing caused by tariff-free imports of mass-produced merchandise from the North, Latino immigrants in the United States contribute their underpaid labor to U.S. capitalism and help sustain the shrinking budget of the U.S. Social Security system with their taxes and payroll deductions.

As one of them wrote shortly before the U.S. mega-march of May Day 2006 by fellow immigrants: "We contribute 25 billion dollars to Social Security and produce some 2 trillion dollars of wealth for the US economy. Without the money generated by this giant composed of 12 million workers labelled illegal and another 36 million legal Hispanics, three important sectors of the economy would be wrecked: services, construction, and manufacturing. . . . The massive mobilizations of immigrants against current immigration policies . . . is a public notice that the sleeping giant has awakened."[2]

The passing of Arizona Senate Bill 1070 (SB 1070) in April 2010, followed by proposals to prohibit ethnic studies programs and instruction by teachers with a strong foreign accent in the state's public schools, did not mark the first time fear has been used to persecute immigrants and divide the working and intermediate classes. Each time an economic recession hits the United States, the capitalists and their mass media try to blame unemployment on immigrants, making them the scapegoats for supposedly "taking jobs from Americans" when actually they "take" relatively few jobs and are either losing their own jobs or being jailed and deported by the hundreds of thousands. U.S. politicians are now accustomed to using these waves of nativism to accumulate votes by warning against "an invasion of illegal foreigners." Under the pretext of combating narco trafficking and terrorism and detaining the flow of illegals, the government militarizes the border, as President Barack Obama continued doing when he deployed 1,200 members of the National Guard to the southwest border in mid-2010

Senate Bill 1070 violated the U.S. Constitution, the Treaty of Guadalupe Hidalgo (United States-Mexico 1848), and the UN's Universal Declaration of Human Rights and its Declaration of the

Rights of Indigenous Peoples. It divided U.S. society. There were many denunciations of the law by city councils from San Francisco to Boston, countless police authorities and organizations, numerous politicians, sports teams, and so on, and at the same time there were proclamations in favor of the law by elements of the same groups. Public opinion polls showed a slight majority in support of SB 1070 but also in favor of a path to legalization for the "illegals." The same polls suggested that anti-immigrant sentiments were strongest among employed white males suffering the effects of the economic recession and elements of the unemployed workforce.

Senate Bill 1070 echoed earlier successful attempts by politicians to garner votes through "immigrant bashing." In 1994, California's governor Peter Wilson got reelected by campaigning for Proposition 187, a referendum focused on the prohibition of education for children of undocumented immigrants. "Prop 187" obtained an overwhelming majority of votes, even though it was later declared unconstitutional. In 2006, the U.S. House of Representatives approved the "Sensenbrenner Law" (HR 4437) that criminalized not only undocumented immigrants but also anyone who in any way offered them moral or material support—doctors, clergy, social workers, and defenders of human rights. A massive, militant, and vigorous social movement of immigrants and their allies eventually defeated HR 4437 in the Senate.

Unfortunately, in almost all the debates on immigration, the words "illegal" and "undocumented" are used to define human beings in a pejorative manner, instead of seeing them as people who *have the right to have rights*. The truth is that today, like yesterday, immigrants to the United States are initially used as "cheap labor" and in that sense have a negative impact on the general wage level. That is why the capitalists and other employers want to import them and exploit them in whatever way possible, whether legal or illegal, sometimes kindly, often cruelly.[3]

In 1996, President Bill Clinton signed the Illegal Immigration Reform and Immigrant Responsibility Act (IIRIRA). This draconian law removed federal courts' jurisdiction for most appeal claims by immigrants, leaving them deportable at the whim of the INS and U.S. Border Patrol agents. It effectively ended due process by exempting from judicial review new government areas whose decisions were no longer appealable, notably "final removal/deportation orders." This was in violation of international treaties governing human rights as well as political refugees. IIRIRA determined that foreigners remaining in the United States without authorization for 180 days to one year or more should be punished, with waiting periods of three to ten years. Moreover, it excluded authorized immigrants from almost all the benefits of Social Security for five years and permanently excluded families of undocumented immigrants from social welfare programs in spite of the taxes they paid into them.

IIRIRA also converted "misdemeanors" into "felonies," thereby creating files filled with "criminal records" that in everyday practice had the effect of negating the rights sought by many people to obtain permission to legally reside and work in the United States. This "felony clause" invalidates the eligibility of those seeking "status adjustment" for spouses, parents, or children of U.S. citizens who upon arrival for their migration interviews are surprised to discover that they have a criminal record that blocks their legalization and subjects them to a process of summary deportation. The same clause affects permanent residents ("green-card holders"), including thousands of U.S. military veterans today known as "Banished Veterans." The IIRIRA's concept of "crime" includes having been deported, overstaying your visa, driving without a license, urinating behind a tree in a park, any minor street or barroom brawl, and is added to an ample catalogue of "migration crimes." Its aftereffects have had a lethal impact on the immigrant population of the United States, especially Mexicans who are living in a veritable humanitarian crisis defined by a growing number of jailed or deported immigrants, divided families, detained children abandoned to their resident community or state social services, not to mention the terror of increased roundups in workplaces, public transportation facilities, Latino neighborhoods, etc.[4]

Moreover, IIRIRA permitted agencies to exchange information and implement pilot programs to verify "elegibility" for employment ("e-verify"). It authorized the U.S. attorney general to arrange written agreements with state and local agencies to carry out functions previously in the exclusive domain of federal immigration personnel, thereby giving rise to local legislative activism that resulted in municipal and state laws that are unconstitutional and anti-immigrant. These agreements, comprising section 287(g) of IIRIRA, are the precedent and basis for such measures as Arizona's SB 1070.

All this is the result of a cluster of initiatives of the Department of Homeland Security (DHS) and its migration arm, Immigration and Customs Enforcement (ICE), sustained by the 1996 laws and empowered by subsequent regulations relating to aspects of "national security" and the "war against terrorism." Mexican immigrants are not terrorists—they have never destroyed a bridge, a building or a house; on the contrary they have built them. "State terrorism," on the other hand, has subjected Latino communities to many hardships, including the loss of life itself. The overwhelming majority of deportees are detained for very minor infractions, without counting the numerous cases of U.S. citizens deported for "looking like an illegal" or for being brown.[5]

The DHS-ICE strategic enforcement plan, implemented by the DHS's Office of Detention and Removal Operations (DRO), is "Operation Endgame," 2003–2012. It "sets in motion a cohesive enforcement program with a ten-year time horizon that will build the capacity to remove all removable aliens."[6] A key part of the strategic plan is the so-called "attrition strategy" that criminalizes and incarcerates many immigrants so that the rest will get the message to leave or not come in the first place. "Operation Secure Streets," "Operation Community Shield," "Operation Verify," and "Secure Communities" are a few elements of this strategy being implemented by DHS-ICE as part of "exhaustive plans to Identify and Remove Criminal Aliens."[7] The intention is "to maximize the long-run return on investment and the success of dissuasion and reduction of recidivism."[8]

The logic of all this, obviously with no respect for the human and labor rights of immigrants, leads to a legalized apartheid system. It reflects an internal political fight in the United States, where the political-electoral strategy of the Republican Party to return to the White House in 2012 is simple: the illegal is a criminal and must be punished. The message is that the United States will lose its identity and culture because of the immigrant "invasion," that the immigrants are going to birth their children in the United States in order to achieve their legalization, that the next U.S. president will be an immigrant, and that the whites will become a minority if immigration is not stopped immediately. In Arizona and other states, Republican legislators are proposing immigration laws that would eliminate the benefits of Social Security, education, housing, and loans, and repeal laws requiring hospitals to provide medical services to the undocumented. They would withdraw federal funding for cities that declare themselves "sanctuaries." Any "brown" person would be subject to detention and deportation.[9]

This systematic tactic—so much to the taste of the Ku Klux Klan, Minute Men, and Hunt-Undocumented—can be compared to what happened in 1850, when the Fugitive Slave Act was passed, with the difference that in today's immigration scene, there is not yet an abundance of "abolitionists" defending basic human rights. It would replicate Jim Crow-type laws used from 1876 to 1965 against the African American community to secure the exclusive rights of whites through racial segregation. The consequences of Arizona's SB 1070 and the propaganda accompanying it will not be erased from the collective consciousness and have already boosted the activism of nativists and neo-Nazis in new right-wing organizations like the influential "Tea Party."[10]

For its part, in June 2010 the Democratic Party adjusted its political strategy on immigration to make it sound more Republican. Obama, who earlier in his presidential campaign referred to immigrants as the undocumented, now calls them illegals, especially when referring to those who will not be covered by the recently approved health care reforms that benefit big insurance and pharmaceutical corporations. Despite his repeated campaign promises, Obama has not carried out his commitment to stop mass deportations and the separation of families. *Every single day* his administration deports 1,000 people, leaving untold numbers of U.S. citizen children to watch a father or mother taken away by men with guns..[11]

The existing political system of the U.S. is uniform and meta-party, and in that sense is a *serpent with two heads* (Democrats and Republicans) whose only real dispute is for political power every four years. Its "Border Patrol" kills Mexican youth even inside Mexican territory, as in the case of Sergio Adrián Hernández in June 2010.[12] And its puppet, de facto president Felipe Calderón, does not order the Mexican army to defend the nation against such aggressive acts but on the contrary orders it to kill more Mexican youths in what is now recognized as a process of *juvenicidio* (youthicide) in the so-called war against drugs.

By not exercising the sovereignty of its people and defending their territorial patrimony but instead governing for a foreign interest, the government of Mexico shows that it does not have the status of a free and sovereign state and constitutes a "failed law." In spite of its rhetorical affirmations of the rights of its emigrants, the fact is that it supports the emigration of its citizens as an "escape valve" for runaway unemployment and the social pressures against it.[13]

The Mexico-U.S. border continues to be a war zone against Mexican and Latin American people, not against terrorism and even less against narco traffickers, who prefer to use airplanes, boats, and banks. U.S. aggression against immigrants, the sending of more troops, and the construction of a wall *larger and worse than any wall in human history* constitute a key part of *the intended fourth conquest of Mexico*, an economic and cultural conquest imposed by neoliberalism and racism (the second intended conquest was the U.S. invasion of 1846–1848 and the third was the French occupation shortly afterwards).

Nowadays in the new constitutions of Latin America, such as that of Ecuador, there are articles that recognize "*the right of persons to migrate. No human being will be identified or considered as illegal because of his/her migratory status*" (Article 40). On the other hand, Mexico continues to mistreat Central American transmigrants, and the United States increases the harassment of Mexicans and Central Americans and the violation of their human rights. For their part, pro-immigrant organizations in the United States continue to mount protests in support of immigration law reform, at times with civil disobedience that echoes the tactics of Martin Luther King and César Chávez during the Civil Rights movements of the 1950s and 1960s. There are national and international calls for an economic boycott against the state of Arizona.

Activists are debating the problematic of whether to support the reelection of Obama. At the same time, they are debating whether to opt for the fight for partial victories, including the "Dream Act" and the "AgJobs Acts" (variations of the failed "Guest Worker Program" of 1942–1965 described by its main administrator as "slavery"), as a kind of consolation prize, since apparently there are no other viable legislative options on the eve of the electoral contests of November 2010.

Several organizations are concentrating their energies on the fight for a moratorium on the massive roundups and for maintaining the unity of millions of "mixed" families composed of citizens and the undocumented. They also call for a reduction and annulment of IIRIRA's 287(g).

Activists achieved a partial victory at the end of July 2010 when a federal judge in Phoenix issued an injunction that blocked the implementation of a few of the key provisions of Arizona's SB 1070, such as "racial profiling," but left intact other criminal activities like harboring undocumented immigrants or impeding traffic by picking up day laborers. Many groups are working for a permanent mobilization and organic organization of the base—the demonstrations and mega-marches—seeking a better coordination between distinct ethnic organizations that already oppose SB 1070 and the countless supportive social movements at an international level. Demands include the repeal of NAFTA, demilitarization of the border, and a reform of immigration laws to make them just and respectful of the civil and labor rights of all persons (in the sense of "Universal Citizenship"). Native American communities along the border continue to play a prominent role in rallying to the defense of immigrant rights and their own ancestral rights. It is their slogan that is repeated in the demonstrations: "We Are Not Illegals, We Are Not Criminals, We Are the Original Peoples."

The "Bill of Rights for the Undocumented Worker" promulgated in Mexico City in April 1980 at the First International Conference for the Full Rights of Undocumented Workers is still valid today.[14] The bill responds to questions commonly asked about what it is that the undocumented want. The reply is simple and always the same: Full Rights for All. The first of the bill's thirteen articles calls for the right to legal residency by simply demonstrating one's status as wage earner and taxpayer. Articles 2 through 11 include the rights guaranteed to citizen workers, such as socioeconomic and labor rights, health and educational services, and the right to practice the culture of one's country of origin. Articles 12 and 13 focus on rights to vote and be voted for in the federal elections of one's native country and U.S. local and state elections, based once again on one's contributions as taxpayer and worker in both countries and one's binationality.

Human mobility is inherent to the process of neoliberal "globalization." Different actors and social groups reproduce inequalities, or find opportunities, in a context of deepening injustices and racial discrimination at a world level and of systemic relations between economic policies and the deterioration of everyday conditions of life. Societies and governments need to recognize that people have a right to migrate and that their fundamental rights migrate with them. No human being should be identified or recognized as "illegal" because of his/her migratory status—this must be universal law.

HUMAN RIGHTS AND FAILED LAW

Sadly, the majority of Mexicans continue suffering violations of their human rights, be it in the United States or in Mexico.[15] As we saw in chapter 2, personnel of the Mexican military and police have committed horrendous crimes against humanity with total impunity but that the world's major human rights organizations have condemned. During the de facto presidency of Calderón, these crimes have included thousands of assassinations, forced disappearances, kidnappings, tortures, and rapes, not to mention the more than 500 new political prisoners who have been subjected to physical and psychological torture. Hardly any of the individuals guilty of these crimes against humanity, or their commanding officers and civilian accomplices, have been punished.

The Mexican state has endorsed international treaties and conventions on human rights but normally ignores them, as does the United States. The government has created its own Comisión Nacional de Derechos Humanos (CNDH) (National Human Rights Commission), but the international institutions that defend human rights or those of Mexican civil society, such as the Organizaciones Indias por los Derechos Humanos en Oaxaca (OIDHO) (Indian Human Rights Organizations of Oaxaca) and the Comité ¡Eureka! (founded by Rosario Ibarra de Piedra in 1977), are much more trustworthy.

Article 22 of the now defunct Constitution of 1917, which prohibits "cruel and unusual punishment, specifically, penalties of death, mutilation, infamy, marks, physical punishments, and torments of any kind," is ignored by the government. Although there are a few good laws that supposedly protect specific groups of the population, there has been little progress—for example, the failure to adequately implement laws on the human rights of the incapacitated.

One of the saddest cases reflecting the impossibility of obtaining justice in Mexico is that of the forty-nine children from eleven months to four years of age who died, and the 104 who were injured, in the famous fire that destroyed the ABC Day Care center, property of the IMSS (Mexican Institute of Social Security in English), in Hermosillo, Sonora, on June 5, 2009. During the years of neoliberalism and privatization, the IMSS had subcontracted almost all the nation's public day care centers to private interests—in the case of ABC Day Care, to an enterprise headed by relatives of Calderón's wife and the state governor. In the ABC tragedy, no one will be punished because the Supreme Court (SCJN, Suprema Corte de Justicia de la Nación) decided in June 2010, by a vote of eight to three, that it is legal to subcontract day care centers to private interests and therefore the court would not decide on responsibilities of those functionaries responsible for the ABC fire but would limit itself to pointing out those "linked" to the violation of guarantees (of adequate care and of life itself). One of the three dissenting justices commented that Mexico remains a country where "everything happens and nothing happens, in which very grave things occur and there are no consequences."[16] The Constitution and all the nation's laws recognize the federal government's obligation in public services like day care centers. In the case of ABC, it appears that the SCJN does not have the competence to punish incompetence.

In truth, there are few instances in which the SCJN shows the competence to make just decisions regarding human rights. During the era of neoliberalism, its justices, appointed by the president and confirmed by the Senate, have received a series of benefits—some people would call them bribes—that have catapulted them to the ranks of the nation's wealthiest. Their official salaries are $50,000 a month, and they receive "extras" equal to thousands more. It is no surprise that the SCJN has ruled that national and local human rights commissions do not have the authority to cite international treaties signed by Mexico when they condemn violations.

The problem with the Mexican courts is the same that affects all high-level public functionaries involved in *la politiquería* (politicking)—the presidency, the congress, and other governmental institutions: a traditional corruption since colonial times that now includes the highest of salaries, kickbacks, and "extras." It is more or less the same in local governments down to the level of municipal mayors. It is one of the reasons behind the impunity of those who commit crimes against humanity.

When the SCJN declared the Cananea strike illegal in February 2010, López Obrador said that Mexico had returned to 1906 and that the rule of law did not exist; the judiciary was under the thumb of the oligarchy. The most central figure in the fight for human rights, Senator Rosario Ibarra, today's president of the Senate's Human Rights Commission and four-time nominee for the Nobel Peace Prize, correctly pointed out that "there are no human rights without the struggles of the peoples, nor is there success for the popular struggles without the defense of human rights."[17]

In the case of the October 10, 2009, midnight military seizure of the para-state enterprise Luz y Fuerza del Centro (LyFC) (Central Light and Power Company of Mexico) and the arbitrary dismissal of 44,000 workers of the Sindicato Mexicano de Electricistas (SME), this writer had the opportunity, as member of civil society's International Tribunal of Trade Union Freedom, to participate in an audience with the Chief Justice of the SCJN. During the one-hour meeting, punctuated by the SME workers' yells for justice from the street below the office, members of our tribunal insisted on a prompt resolution of the SME's justly filed *amparo* (stay or suspension of the takeover and firing, and the immediate reinstallation of the workers in their jobs) because existing labor laws and the Constitution had been so flagrantly violated. Moreover, the dozens of SME members on a hunger strike since April 2010 could not last much longer. The tribunal's delegation noted that labor rights are human rights, and both had been violated in this case. After commenting that this was the final instance in the courts for resolving the problem, we explained that a denial by the Supreme Court of the SME's *amparo* would represent the effective end of the tripartite division of powers between the three governmental institutions and might trigger a social explosion in Mexico, and globally would result in an additional loss of respect for Mexico and its "failed law." The Chief Justice observed that "this is an activist court," but after the meeting we commented that "the judicial activism" of this court always had been in favor of the government and private capital, not of the workers.[18]

On July 7, 2010, the SCJN ruled on the SME *amparo*. It sustained the constitutionality of the military's and Calderón's actions against the union, but recognized the SME as the legitimate rerpresentative of the workers and left the door open for it to return to the Federal Labor Board to demand reinstatement for its members. The hunger strikers rejected the SCJN decision, declaring that "the constitutional order is broken and the rule of law has been violated." Not long afterwards, when a new secretary of government expressed for the first time an openness to negotiations, they ended their hunger strike on its eighty-ninth day. The SME reiterated its demands: that the Federal Commission of Electricity (the national electric company) hire the 17,000 workers who had rejected the government compensation packages; its determination to maintain nonviolent struggle and to unify all democratic forces; and its ongoing mobilization for a general strike to be coordinated with the one scheduled in Europe for September 29, 2010.

On June 28, 2010, in another world-famous case of an *amparo* involving human rights violations, the SCJN ordered the release of twelve political prisoners who had been incarcerated since May of 2006 for having led and participated in the nonviolent protests that blocked the building of an international airport on the *ejidal* lands of San Salvador Atenco outside Mexico City. They had resisted the police takeover of their lands in Atenco, which had led to the killing of one youth, the arrest and kidnapping of 240 people, and the rape of twenty-eight women by police personnel. The government's own CNDH and various magistrates had condemned the multiple human rights violations during the police raid of Atenco and declared the prisoners innocent of the charges against them. Nonetheless, the twelve political prisoners received absurdly long sentences, including one of 112 years for Ignacio del Valle, the leader of the Popular Front for the Defense of the Land.

Another recent Supreme Court decision freed three Otomi Indian women serving twenty-one-year sentences for allegedly kidnapping six Federal Investigative Agency employees harassing an Indian market in the state of Queretaro. In most cases the SCJN has ruled against the rights of the original peoples, such as its ruling upholding the government's breaking of the San Andrés Accords negotiated by the EZLN in 2002; and in 2009, it freed prisoners accused of the Acteal massacre in Chiapas in 1997. On the other hand, the Supreme Court recently upheld the constitutionality of the new law permitting same-sex marriage in the Federal District (DF).

Violations of Mexico's Constitution in the numerous cases of professional journalists whose human rights have been violated are by now legendary. The independent reporter Laura Castellanos, victim of the government's tapping of her telephone and other acts of illegal surveillance of her person, her computer, and her domicile, affirmed in a letter to the daily newspaper *La Jornada* on May 30, 2010, that 65 percent of aggressive acts against the nation's journalists in 2009 were perpetrated by the state. She ended her letter with these words: "I hold the government of Felipe Calderón responsible for any act against my integrity or that of my family. I go on with my pen in hand."

Famous examples of murders of journalists, with impunity for their assassins, include the deaths of Manuel Buendía of the prestigious newspaper *Excélsior* in 1984 and Brad Will of *Indymedia New York City* in 2006. Will was assassinated while filming the protests of the Popular Assembly of the Peoples of Oaxaca (APPO) during the inspirational days of "the commune of Oaxaca."[19]

The extrajudicial executions and sieges of the communities of the original peoples of Oaxaca and other parts of the nation continue with impunity.[20] They have been extended to people who try to bring them material aid. On April 27, 2010, a paramilitary group, created in 1994 by the Oaxacan government of the PRI, opened fire on a caravan of at least twenty-five observers from Mexico and Europe and two Mexican journalists that was heading for the autonomous municipality of San Juan Copala in the Triqui region of Oaxáca. Two human rights activists were killed: Beatriz Alberta Cariño Trujillo of Mexico and Jyri Jaakkola of Finland (whose murder was officially protested by the Finnish government and the European Union). Several members of the caravan were wounded and a few managed to escape into the mountains.

Almost a month later the leader of the Independent Triqui Movement of Unification and Struggle (MULTI), Timoteo Alejandro Ramírez and his wife, Tleriberta Castro Aguilar, were murdered at close range in Yosoyuxi, Oaxaca. In June, a second humanitarian caravan of 300 persons including members of

Congress had to detour when the paramilitaries started shooting. Local and federal police stood by and did nothing. Not long after the defeat of the criminal PRI governor in the July elections by a candidate of the PRD backed by the PAN, preparations for an even larger caravan were under way with people from the Red Cross and the United Nations. The same paramilitaries then invaded San Juan Copala and took control of its 500 families.[21]

The absence of governmental authority in regions like the Triqui is not only another indication of "failed law" but also a proof of the complicity of the state and its institutions in the elimination of activists and potentially of entire peoples, that is, ethnocide. It is *governability by force, against the law*—and the majority of the population is aware of that.

Meanwhile, the rhythm of feminicide and youthicide mentioned earlier continues to accelerate. The Childhood Network in Mexico (Redim) has noted that the government refers to "collateral damage" in its "battle against organized crime." Redim demands an accurate and regular record of civilian deaths, especially with regard to minors under eighteen years of age, whether victims or authors of crimes connected to the so-called war against drugs, "with the data broken down by sex, age, state and municipality."[22] In Ciudad Juárez alone, the government has left more than 10,000 orphans and half of the youth without schooling or jobs. There is almost total impunity; 90 percent of the murders are not even investigated. Mexico's young people from the lower and intermediate classes are feeling angry and fearful about the new phenomenon of youthicide. In the eyes of many authorities, to be young is to be criminal. Many young people from broken families or without job opportunities, or fed up with the obstacles to a better future, look for other solutions. Some emigrate, but they are doing so in smaller numbers during these years of economic recession, militarization of the border, and intensified attacks against Mexicans in the United States. The majority enter the army or criminal bands where the pay is much better than what is offered in the few jobs they might find. Moreover, there is a high rate of desertions from the army because the soldiers receive better offers from the narcos with whom they often feel safer.[23]

Human rights include labor rights, which in Mexico are also disappearing under the iron fist of the current government.[24] In 2009, six workers defending their rights were assassinated, and almost all workers suffer frontal attacks by the authorities, similar to the ones experienced by the miners and electrical workers. Even so, the popular resistance movements persevere. There is also a special crisis involving the human and labor rights of the elderly. The social security reforms and other neoliberal policies like taxes on pensions threaten them. Their health services are being reduced and the costs of their medicines are increasing. Provision of special social, cultural, and economic services is ending. Therefore, in June 2010, the First National Assembly of the Retired and Pensioned decided to incorporate the elderly into the process of popular resistance movements rocking the nation.

NATURE'S RIGHTS

While the most industrialized countries, led by the United States, mercantilize the life and goods of *Madre Tierra*, other forces in the world insist on alternatives like those listed in the "Agreement of the Peoples" approved in April 2010 by 35,000 persons from 140 nations during the "World Conference of the Peoples on Climate Change and the Rights of Madre Tierra," convoked by Bolivia's president Evo Morales in Cochabamba.[25] The alternatives include: a universal declaration of the rights of Nature; an international tribunal on climatic justice; the most industrialized nations' honoring of their "climatic debt"; and a worldwide popular referendum on climate change.

The Agreement of the Peoples echoed the slogan shouted by some 100,000 demonstrators at the Youth Climate Forum of

Copenhagen in December 2009: "Don't change the climate, change the system!" It concluded that there exists "a terminal crisis of the patriarchal civilizing model based on the subjugation and destruction of human beings and nature that escalated with the industrial revolution" and that the capitalist, colonialist, and imperalist systems must be replaced by "a new system that reestablishes harmony with nature and among human beings." It rejected free trade agreements and supported the recognition of water as a "fundamental human right." In its eight detailed pages, it noted the existence of 50 million climatic immigrants and projections for the year 2050 of "from 200 million to a billion persons who will be displaced by situations brought about by climate change."[26]

For its part, in 2010 Mexico's broad coalition, Asamblea Nacional de Afectados Ambientales (ANAA) (National Assembly of Environmentally Affected), warned of an environmental disaster resulting from "the destructive role of transnational corporations and the most diversified authorities of the Mexican government, as much from the sacking and looting of strategic resources and community rights as from the destruction caused by environmental laws, the corruption of systems of governmental vigilance, or the complicity, corruption and impunity with which they act." ANAA cited as one of the problems the repression carried out by a nondemocratic state.[27]

The Partido Verde Ecologista de Mexico (PVEM) (Green Ecologist Party of Mexico), founded in 1986, is right-wing and neoliberal. It has participated in the politicking of forming alliances with the PAN and more recently with the PRI. The PVEM does not have a good record in defense of the environment. In 2008, the Mexican government tried to permit foreign consortia like British Petroleum (BP), which has huge investments from U.S. corporations and banks, to exploit the underwater sources of crude oil located in Mexico's deepest territorial waters, but a militant social movement in defense of the Constitution's protection of oil blocked the attempt. After the recent ecological disaster caused by BP in the Gulf of Mexico, it is obvious that the semi-privatization of Mexico's oil and gas, together with the almost complete privatization of mining, granting concessions equivalent to 12 percent of the national territory, is putting the environment and the health of millions of people at risk.

Environmental problems in Mexico caused by capitalism and its consumerist culture are extremely serious and violate the rights of nature and of environmental activists. Some examples:

- The contamination of waters, lands, and communities by foreign companies in the agricultural and livestock industry as in the case of the A/H1N1 influenza pandemic of 2009 that originated in the state of Veracruz and, as revealed later by the director of the World Health Organization (WHO), resulted in billions of dollars of income for transnational pharmaceutical corporations that had connections with members of the WHO's emergency committee.[28]

- The effects in general of the drive by transnational agro-industry and its producers of agrochemical products to generate agro-exports, including new megaplantations of palm oil for the production of biocombustibles, that often destroy forests and leave some states looking like lunar landscapes.

- The contamination of waters, lands, and communities by the largely privatized mining industry, including threats to ecosystems, like that of Minera San Xavier (MSX), a subsidiary of the Canadian firm New Gold Inc. in the region of Cerro de San Pedro, San Luis Potosí, being fought by an international coalition that includes Mexico's Frente Amplio Opositor a Minera San Xavier (FAO).

- The contamination of rivers, lakes, and lagoons, leading to the disappearance of species of fish and birds, as is happening in the lagoon of Zumpango, state of Mexico.

- The privatization of the lands of the original peoples by the ecotourist industry that threatens archeological zones and their environments, such as in Chiapas, Chichén Itzá, and Teotihuacán.

- The murders of environmental activists among the original peoples such as Mariano Abarca Roblero (or even mayors as in the case of Cerro de San Pedro) and the detention of organizers who oppose the consortia of Mexican, Canadian, U.S., and European companies responsible for so much destruction.

- The proposal to help solve the climate crisis by geoengineering the use of transgenic products that are super shiny to deflect the rays of the sun (Monsanto's transgenic seeds are already destroying the environment).

- The collapse of ecosystems as in the case of the Río Santiago—"the river of death"—that receives the residue and waste of numerous industrial centers in the El Salto region in the state of Jalisco.

- The health problems and environmental damage caused by out-of-control urbanization.

- The destructive impact of megaprojects like Plan Puebla Panamá or the construction of industrial *maquiladora* zones and immense dams like the hydroelectric reservoir at La Parota, Guerrero, one of several poorly designed programs denounced by the Interamerican Association for the Defense of the Environment.

- The dumping of toxic wastes in Mexico from San Diego and other parts of the United States.

- The threat of an irreparable drought in less than twenty years.

- The current Mexican government has even more plans to privatize the environment. According to "Plan México 2030, Proyecto de Gran Visión," described in chapter 2, there are Projects of Provision of Services (PPS), public works, and concessions of multiple service contracts included in the "Uma," or conservation units for wildlife habitat. At least twenty-three biosphere reserves have already been partially privatized under the rubric of the Uma, according to official reports by the Secretariat of Environment and Natural Resources. As anthropologist Gilberto López y Rivas has observed, "This entails 2 million and 456,142 hectares of 'protected natural habitats' in the hands of private interests, by means of 66 conservation units of the Uma."[29]

POLITICKING, RESISTANCE MOVEMENTS, AND INTERNATIONALISM

Polls in 2010 show that 70 percent of students refuse to vote, even though one's electoral card serves as an identity card for cashing a check and other routine tasks. The political system in Mexico, like the one in the United States, is metaparty, a *serpent with two heads*: the PAN and the PRI, or in most state policies the PRIAN. In both Mexico and the United States, we have been witnessing since September 11, 2001, an "introduction of dictatorship by stages."[30] The Mexican serpent practices a form of rotation of the presidency and faithfully implements the infamous imperialist "*planes*" described in chapter 2. Whether before or after the opening of the neoliberal era in 1982, Mexican voters have long realized their votes are futile. Consequently, in most elections the "winner" has always been abstentionism.

The most popular political coalition during two of the national electoral campaigns has been composed of ex-Priistas and groups of the center and left. It generated the birth of the PRD. But that unstable coalition suffered two stolen presidential elections (in 1988 and 2006) and several internal splits. For July 2010's regional elections, the PRD formed alliances with the PAN in select states to attempt defeat of the PRI. This strategy received strong criticism by López Obrador, the "legitimate president" who won the robbed election of 2006. With the exception of López Obrador and his *brigadistas* and *Adelitas*, the PRD, like the PAN and the PRI, represents opportunism and corruption.

Mexico's small left-wing parties, despite their important contributions to social movements and strikes, have not received a sufficient number of votes in recent years to qualify for participation in elections. For example, the Partido Revolucionario de los Trabajadores (PRT), a Trotskyist formation that won 4 to 8 percent of the vote in 1982 when it backed Doña Rosario Ibarra, the first woman ever to run for the presidency, always has had a significant influence in the fight for democratic trade unions and the second wave of the feminist movement. Many leftist organizations continue to suffer the blows of the system of repression and cooptation described in chapter 3. Government agents regularly infiltrate leftist and pro-democracy groups where they often act as "ultras" to create a lack of trust in the public. (There are also genuine "ultras" on the left who have the same negative impact.) The Mexican left is fragmented and weak, but two parties, the Partido del Trabajo (PT) and the Partido Convergencia, have allied with López Obrador and become members of the PRD in the new "Dialogue for the Reconstruction of Mexico" (DIA) founded in December 2009.

The neo-Zapatistas have sympathizers throughout the world, but their actual power in Mexico is limited to Chiapas and a few isolated parts of other southern and central states where each autonomous municipality frequently confronts a military and paramilitary encirclement, San Juan Copala-style. That is one reason why in July 2010 the Zapatistas undertook a campaign to stop the harassment of their communities, called "Campaign thousands of angers, one heart: long live the Zapatista communities!"[31]

Many people within and outside of Mexico's vigorous social movements believe that the party system is not politically viable and that honest elections are impossible. The presidential contests in Mexico are the most expensive in the world; the estimated cost for the 2012 campaign exceeds one billion dollars.

This notwithstanding, López Obrador believes in the possibility of the electoral road. After his official defeat in 2006, he travelled throughout the country to organize a nonviolent movement "from below" and established hundreds of local support committees. More than two million citizens registered as representatives of López Obrador's "Legitimate Government" and its committment to the fight for the transformation of the country.

In June 2010, López Obrador presented his book, *La mafia que se adueñó de Mexico . . . y el 2012* (The Mafia that Took Over Mexico . . . and 2012). He compared it with Francisco I. Madero's *La sucesión presidencial* (1908), written like his own book two years before presidential elections. In both books the authors appeal to "all good Mexicans." In his book, López Obrador affirmed that it was very possible the Left would suffer another electoral defeat in 2012 and that it didn't matter if the Left chose him or another responsible person as its candidate, such as his friend Marcelo Ebrard Casaubón "who skillfully governs Mexico City." The important thing, concluded López Obrador, is that "the revolution in consciences to construct the new republic is already under way."[32]

At his press conferences in 2010 López Obrador often said about the "Mafia in power" and the next presidential elections: "We are going to defeat them and we will achieve the transformation of the country with the citizenry's organization and the mobilization of the people." He also recognized that the oligarchy controls the Federal Electoral Institute (IFE), the Electoral Tribunal of the Judicial Power of the Federation (TEPJF), and "the majority of the mass media and especially television." Moreover, he acknowledged that a democracy is not possible in Mexico "so long as the all-embracing power of Televisa exists" and that "the only way out for Mexico is an authentic and profound social and political revolution."[33]

On July 25, 2010, López Obrador declared to a packed Zócalo plaza in Mexico City that he was seeking the presidency in 2012 with what he called "an alternative project for the nation" with the help of a growing social movement "from below." He reiterated his ten-point reformist program that had first appeared in *Regeneración*, January 2010. Many of Mexico's social movements and popular assemblies championed welfare-state type reforms similar to López Obrador's ten points. In fact, the ninth point of his program called explicitly for a "welfare state."

There are other influential politicians in the wings whose futures are unclear. One is Cuauhtémoc Cárdenas, winner of the stolen election of 1988. He has, at times, been critical of neoliberalism and the PRD. Another is a leader and ex-presidential candidate of the PAN, Diego Fernández de Cevallos, one of Mexico's wealthiest individuals who mysteriously disappeared in May 2010, apparently kidnapped. Theories abound as to what happened to him, but he may yet reappear as the "savior" of his party that did poorly in the July 2010 elections. Then there is the still powerful ex-president, Carlos Salinas de Gortari (1988–1994). According to López Obrador and other analysts, Salinas controls much of the political power in Mexico through the network of millionaires and politicians whose careers he helped launch.[34]

One thing is abundantly clear: the political culture analyzed in chapter 3 continues very much alive and all the political parties running candidates in elections have adopted the style of the PRI. As journalist Marco Rascón says, "The PRI is in every cell of our body politic. . . . It's in the Left, the Right and the Center; in the unions, in the renewed control, in the business leadership."[35]

In a militarized society nothing is easy, whether it be electoral campaigning or popular mobilization "from below." All the resistance groups and social movements have experienced many defeats in the last decades. Nevertheless, popular resistance has grown since October 2009, sparked by the militant activists of the Mexican Electrical Workers Union (SME), the Miners' Union, the National Coordinating Committee of Education Workers (CNTE), the original peoples, and leftist groups like the Feministas Socialistas (FS). In mid-2010, the CNTE was maintaining a sit-in at various national governmental offices in greater Mexico City as the government continued to fail to respond to its demands. Hunger strikes had been launched in various parts of the nation, including the overcrowded and dangerous prisons, and numerous groups were carrying out nonviolent acts of civil disobedience.[36]

In addition, there are signs of new social movements among young people, although the biggest gatherings continue to be the outdoor music concerts that attract up to 100,000 people. In Oaxaca, Nuevo León, Mexico City and other parts of the nation, university students have been protesting the conditions that threaten their futures, especially educational budget cuts and tuition increases. In many states, students at the rural "normal" schools that train future schoolteachers defend themselves against the government's proposals to shut them down. For many rural children the normal schools have traditionally been the only avenue open to them for improving their lot. The independent unions of Latin America's largest university, the Universidad Nacional Autónoma de México (UNAM), maintain their resistance against proposals to privatize education and often join the CNTE, the SME, and other activists in the massive street demonstrations.

Many activists fight for a new *constituyente* (constitutional assembly) to write a new Constitution. Various groups and individuals among the anti-neoliberal forces advocate a strategy that combines a focus on the social and labor movements with participation in select elections, always with the objective of achieving a true revolutionary change in society. In this sense it is possible to support "the other campaign" of the neo-Zapatistas, which rejects electoral activity, and simultaneously work with all the anti-neoliberal forces to push them toward the new revolution that Mexico needs.[37]

The internationalist vision the Magonistas represented a century ago has surfaced anew among Mexican workers inside and outside of the country. It has contributed to recent victories of struggles by workers seeking independent and democratic unions, like the one achieved by the rubber workers of Hulera Euzkadi S.A. de C.V. described in the opening chapter and the May 2010 success of the 342 auto workers at the Johnson Controls plant (Resurección) in Puebla. With backing from several international labor confederations, these auto workers—who produce component parts for Mercedes-Benz, BMW, Nissan, Chrysler, and Volkswagen—conducted a militant strike that won the cancellation of a protection contract and recognition of their independent union with a more favorable contract.

In several international meetings, such as the U.S. Social Forum in late June 2010, Mexico's independent trade unionists have contributed and received considerable solidarity. For example, during Mexico's alternative summit organized to coincide with the G20 in Toronto in June 2010, activists dedicated an entire day of exploration to "BUILDING SOLIDARITY WITH THE DEMOCRATIC TRADE UNION MOVEMENT OF MEXICO." Napoleón Gómez Urrutia and Martín Esparza, the leaders of the independent miners' and electrical workers' unions, participated in workshops sponsored by the Continental Social Alliance. Meanwhile, civil society's International Tribunal of Trade Union Freedom has commenced internal discussions on how to expand its mission as a Tribunal Internacional Permanente de Libertad Sindical (TIPLS).

The SME has gained the active support of diverse labor organizations, including the International Trade Union Confederation, the world's largest trade union bloc representing 166 million workers in 156 nations. Mexico's miners have also received the backing of international trade union organizations, such as: the International Metalworkers' Federation; the International Federation of Chemical, Energy, Mining and General Workers' Unions; the International Brotherhood of Teamsters; the Canadian Labour Congress; and the AFL-CIO and the United Steelworkers (USW, of the United States, Canada, and the Caribbean). Talks of mergers are under way between the USW, which represents 850,000 workers, and Mexico's independent Miners' Union of 180,000 workers. USW president Leo W. Gerard has condemned Calderón for having launched "a reign of terror against Cananea's workers." The USW is pressuring the U.S. Congress to stop sending funds to Mexico's security forces since they can be used "to attack workers who exercise their right to freedom of association."[38]

In March 2010, the Committee on Trade Union Freedom of the International Labor Organization (ILO) responded to a complaint filed by the International Metalworkers' Federation. The ILO committee declared that the Mexican government had violated the ILO's conventions 87 and 98 on trade union freedom and the right to collective bargaining by using the army and the police to break strikes, kill workers, and detain union leaders. The ILO urged the government to negotiate a resolution of the conflict in Cananea and to reply to a complaint filed at the ILO by the SME. It is possible that in 2011 Mexico will be placed on the

ILO's blacklist of the twenty-five countries with the most severe violations of international labor conventions.[39]

The upsurge in internationalism is strong in the immigrants' movement as well. The Southwest Workers Union is one of many grassroots organizations in the United States backing the internationalization of the fight for the rights of immigrants. The AFL-CIO, whose heretofore shrinking membership has grown a bit through the recruitment of immigrants, has repeatedly condemned Arizona's SB 1070. In June 2010, AFL-CIO president Richard Trumka, the son of European immigrants, gave a speech criticizing the militarization of the border, NAFTA, proposed programs of "guest workers," and the badmouthing of immigrants, especially the false accusation that "immigrants are taking our jobs." Trumka said: "When I hear that kind of talk, I want to say, did an immigrant move your plant overseas? Did an immigrant take away your pension? Or cut your health care? Did an immigrant destroy American workers' right to organize? Or crash the financial system? Did immigrant workers write the trade laws that have done so much harm to Ohio?" Trumka added: "There was no labor movement in America until workers learned to look at each other and see not immigrants and native born, not white and black, not different last names, but our common fate as workers." He connected the problematics of immigration to labor rights, the right to vote, and the greed of businesspeople who feed on cheap labor. "Our economic strategy," he affirmed, "must bring us together instead of driving us apart . . . an economic strategy for shared prosperity based on rising wages in both countries. . . . We have learned through our history that it is only when working people stand together—in the workplace and at the polling place—that the American Dream is secure."[40]

On May 29, 2010, some 100,000 persons marched in Phoenix, Arizona, against SB 1070, while 3,000 demonstrated in a similar fashion in front of the American embassy in Mexico City. Solidarity with Mexican and other immigrants has been part of the work of the first International Tribunal of Conscience of Peoples in Movement that will continue its drive in the first week of November 2010 as part of an alternative forum to the "IV Foro Mundial sobre Migración y Desarrollo" (Fourth World Forum on Migration and Development) organized by the Mexican government and the BBVA Bancomer Foundation.[41]

One hundred years ago, Ricardo Flores Magón insisted that without a praxis of internationalism, a revolution in the interests of the men and women who produce the wealth—that is, the working classes of the countryside and the city—is not possible. Many activists believe that Mexico requires a revolution to emerge from its loss of sovereignty and democracy and to eliminate the ubiquitous corruption. How to achieve this Herculean task, or at least prepare the ground for such a radical change, is the subject of ongoing debates in today's Mexico.

CONCLUSION

Reactivate the Revolutionary Fight!

> In this march we Zapatistas also have been part of the rebellious Mexicos, of seeing ourselves and seeing the others. That, and nothing else, is "la dignidad" [dignity]. The Mexicos of below, particularly the indigenous, tell us a story of struggle and resistance that comes from afar and now beats in each place. Yes, but it is a story that looks ahead.
>
> —SUBCOMANDANTE MARCOS[1]

> A predatory oligarchy oppresses and dominates Mexico. . . unlike the *Porfiriato* or the governments of the PRI that based their power on the use of the firm hand and the predominance of a single party, this group asserts its authority, basically, by the control it exerts over the mass media.
>
> —ANDRÉS MANUEL LÓPEZ OBRADOR[2]

The lessons of the "modernization" strategies in a capitalist Mexico dominated by foreigners are clear: neither the liberalism of the "Científicos" in the era of Porfirio Díaz nor the neoliberalism of the contemporary technocratic thieves based on an oil monoculture and foreign investment has been able to provide economic well-being or security for Mexico's citizenry.

Mexico has abundant wealth in natural and human resources but its economic and political system is completely corrupt and at the service of U.S. imperialism. Neoliberal governments have privatized most sectors of the economy and reduced the Mexican state's role to "repressive apparatus." NAFTA and related neoliberal policies have left the economy without a dynamic internal market for local products and extreme socioeconomic inequalities. Except for narco exports, the main sources of national income have suffered reverses in the twenty-first century, including the sale of oil and gas, tourism, immigrant remittances, and the *maquila* assembly plants.

Mexico's architects of neoliberalism—who do not confront the low-wage basis of incomplete industrialization but rather try to take advantage of it—have built a castle of sand propped up by the dollars of narco-trafficking and the guns of imperialism. They have mortgaged the country and its huge reserve of inexpensive labor power to foreigners. Mexico has transferred unprecedented amounts of capital to the United States—not only in terms of its natural resources and "value added" by labor at the points of production, but also in the literal transfer of almost a fifth of its labor force.[3]

In the year of the centenary of the Mexican Revolution, comparisons to the conditions of 1910 have invariably been made. The planet is in full climatic crisis; "limited" nuclear war is a real possibility; and most of the world remains in a prolonged structural economic recession produced by neoliberal capitalism. Latin America—except for the puppet states of imperialism like Mexico, Honduras, and Colombia—is beginning to organize itself as a distinct power bloc with its own way of confronting the economic crisis, independent of imperialism's international financial institutions and dollar monopoly in world commerce and currency exchanges. In 2011, a new political organization of the entire region will step onto the world stage: the Organization of Latin American and Caribbean States.

For its part, the U.S. government is ratcheting up its military response. It has increased the budget for its Special Forces, which are free to act as death squads in more than sixty nations and could be used during any greater crisis in Mexico. But U.S. imperialism is incapable of winning militarily anywhere, neither the wars in Iraq and Afghanistan nor the so-called war against drugs (which it is not interested in winning in the first place, as we saw in chapter 2). It cannot resolve the problematic of immigration either. It is an empire in decline, inundated with problems that imperialism itself has created.

Mexico is a key link in U.S. imperialism's plans to gain control over the world's energy, biosphere, and mineral and water resources. But it is a "weak link," as events dating from the 1988 presidential election have suggested. The current Mexican government's record of war, death, and accelerated immiseration of the masses has caused even Washington to start distancing itself from de facto president Felipe Calderón.[4]

The situation in Mexico is very complex and unstable. Most of the social movements and independent trade unions have left the political parties behind and become the main force for a radical and even revolutionary change. They say they are ready to negotiate, but the government doesn't negotiate; on the contrary it represses. Therefore, say some activists, it's time to create more communities of resistance and self-government on the way to taking control of the government—by no means easy, but certainly possible as the peoples of Bolivia and other countries have shown.

Although the word "socialism" is not frequently heard, the reformist and transitional demands of the social and labor movements almost always include the word "revolution," normally in the sense of transforming or reconstructing society in a process that is pacific, unifying, democratic, constructive, self-generating, nationalist, and internationalist, often with the ideas of libertarian socialism and anarcho-communism championed by Ricardo Flores Magón.[5] At the same time, there are constant references to the glorious moments of rebellion in Mexican history. In the words of López Obrador, "What is more dignified for a Mexican than to follow the example of Hidalgo, Morelos, Juárez, Madero, Villa, Zapata, Flores Magón and General Lázaro Cárdenas."[6] As an SME flier states: "The triumphs of the Revolution are our heritage and are not negotiable." Historian Adolfo Gilly speaks of the genealogy of rebellions being "not to repeat but to receive, enrich and renovate the immaterial legacy that they left us."[7] And that is what Mexico's activists are trying to do in 2010 in the face of almost insurmountable obstacles.

There is a rich diversity and sad fragmentation of the democratic forces, and there is a possibility, and certainly a necessity, of unifying them. Everyone realizes that a new political culture must be created, one based on the values of solidarity instead of individualism, of honesty instead of corruption, and of an ethics that incorporates the ideals of all Mexico's historic rebellions and not their betrayal that is also part of the heritage. People know they have to replace the fear the current government has generated with the antithesis of fear: audacity.[8]

Common sense tells us that if today's economic globalization is imperialism—that is, the expansion of monopoly capital, principally of the United States, backed by quite superior military power—then the only solution to problems created by globalization is the socialization of those large enterprises of monopoly capitalism and their subsidiaries in Mexico and other parts of the world. Only new anticapitalist alternatives and internationalist alliances can overcome such strong obstacles, be it in Mexico or the United States itself. Only profound changes can open roads to new systems. As Mexico's world-renowned sociologist Pablo González Casanova has stated, "It is naïve to think that capitalism will resolve the world's problems."[9]

It also may be naïve to think that a transition to a new system can be achieved without the use of violence. Young Mexican activists look at the bourgeoisie's reaction to radical peaceful change with overwhelming military might and bloodshed and ask: "Isn't an armed popular struggle needed?" After all, look at what happened in Salvador Allende's Chile on September 11, 1973. I always tell these young activists that in my opinion this does not appear to be an appropriate moment to promote an armed rebellion the way the Magonistas did in 1906–1911. The circumstances are different, above all the inequality of military power between the citizenry and the armed forces of Mexico and the United States. But if the nonviolent movements do not win a few victories in the short and intermediate run, it's quite likely that urban or rural guerrilla units will launch some violent actions, as they have done in the past. Assuming some degree of popular support, in order to win, the advocates of armed struggle would have to gain the support of members of the military, or at least divide them. That would require organizing a political strategy prior to any armed action and making contact with soldiers who come from the lower classes and officers of a "patriotic" bent.[10]

One thing is clear: there are no easy or obvious solutions when so many factors are complicating the situation nationally and internationally. Now is an opportune time to think of resolving social justice issues not at the state level but at an *international* level, as Flores Magón did. Even as the creators of injustice strategize beyond borders, so must we. Through the praxis of international mutual support and coordination of social struggles, there is a greater chance of winning substantial victories and simultaneously avoiding the marginalization of trans-border injustices like those affecting the migrants, or the victims of the drug wars, or divided families and children, or the rights of the original peoples, women, and other social minorities.[11]

Advancing this internationalism is both possible and necessary. Whether in Mexico or the United States, regressive taxes, salary cuts, job layoffs, slashed budgets for public services, and inflated costs of education and other necessities are savaging the working and intermediate classes. Politicians and conservatives, abetted by the mass media, are using the consequent anger and desperation of millions of people to strengthen an international right-wing offensive.[12]

Activists in both countries need to deepen the nascent anti-imperialist coalition that showed itself in the Mexican immigrants' mega-march of May Day 2006 and the immigrant marches of 2010 when social, labor, and human rights movements on both sides of the border began to unite. The more that the social and labor movements on both sides of the U.S.-Mexico border link up, and the more that the world's social movements join forces, the greater will be the challenges to U.S. imperialism and for the hope of humanity. The two key words are *internationalism* and *unity*.

This means thinking, imagining, and building nationally and internationally—through conferences and popular assemblies offering opportunities for dialogue and respect for differences—a new libertarian socialism, pluralist and democratically participatory, that in the case of Indo-Afro-Latin America must and can be, as the great Peruvian revolutionary José Carlos Mariátegui explained in 1928, "neither an exact replica nor a copy of anything but something heroically determined in the popular struggles of the peoples in each country and internationally."[13] Such a creative process is already under way in a growing number of countries, at uneven but ever more combined levels. In brief, we need to continue the democratic development of an anti-neoliberal, anti-capitalist, anti-imperialist, pro-indigenous and anti-patriarchal program within an internationalist framework.[14]

In 2010, Mexico celebrates the bicentenary of the start of its independence movement from Spain in September and the centenary of the start of the Mexican Revolution in November. In the Mayan calendar, the year 2012 is the year of the great "cyclical turn," that is, the end of this human civilization and the start of a new one. The future of the planet and humanity is at risk. Without the continuous daily work of many people in different countries organizing new revolutionary processes against the capitalist system and imperialism, there will not be a new civilization or that newly possible and indispensable world for which so many millions of people hope and speak. There is not much time left to reactivate the revolutionary fight, but I am certain that, as has happened so often in Mexican history, the dignity of Mexico's women and men will yet again vanquish fear and death and play a crucial role in this "change of epoch."

Los pueblos unidos jamás serán vencidos.
The peoples united will never be defeated.

Manos a la obra, pues.
Let's get down to work, then.

—JAMES D. COCKCROFT, Montréal, Québec, Canada,
Otro Mundo, August 15, 2010

Notes

INTRODUCTION

1. See cover of Armando Bartra, *Regeneración 1900–1918* (México, D.F.: Queromón Editores, 1972).

CHAPTER ONE: MEXICANS RISE UP, 1910–2010: SIMILARITIES AND DIFFERENCES

1. There is no "middle class." There are "intermediate classes," as defined and explained in James D. Cockcroft, *Mexico's Hope* (New York: Monthly Review Press, 1998), 50–54.
2. The interrelationship between various narcotraffickers and high officials of the Mexican government is well known. Former president Miguel de la Madrid states that his successor Salinas de Gortari maintained intimate links with the narcos. Drug czar General Jesús Gutiérrez Rebollo was arrested in 1997 for having protected the Juárez Cartel. Today there are similar accusations against Ginaro García Luna, the head of the *Secretaría de Seguridad Pública* (SSP) (Public Security Secretariat) which is responsible for the Policía *Federal Preventiva* (PFP) (Federal Preventative Police), renowned for its repression of social activists.
3. As the Flores Magón brothers and their allies in the Partido Liberal Mexico (PLM) (Mexican Liberal Party) were called.
4. Their mother nevertheless insisted that the boys be educated in Mexico City—had not the Oaxacan Indian Benito Juárez advanced

himself in that manner? However, the Flores Magón brothers, with the exception of Jesús who finished his legal training, never had sufficient funds to complete their formal education and ended up taking menial jobs and becoming revolutionaries. All three developed their anarchist and socialist ideas before the founding of the PLM, but Ricardo was by far the most prominent of the three in leadership, theory, and practice.

5. James D. Cockcroft, *Intellectual Precursors of the Mexican Revolution* (Austin: University of Texas Press, 1968, and Albuquerque: University of New Mexico Press, 2010), 75.
6. *Ejidos* are the traditional communal landholdings of the original peoples.
7. See Armando Bartra, *Regeneración 1900–1918* (México, D.F.: Queromón Editores, 1972), 283–286.
8. Bartra, 289–292. It should be noted that *Regeneración*, despite the persecution of its writers and readers, maintained a clandestine circulation of 30,000 copies! The newspaper was financed almost entirely by small donations from Mexican workers.
9. See Vicki Ruíz and Virginia Sánchez Korrol, eds., *Latinas in the United States: A Historical Encyclopedia* (Bloomington: Indiana University Press, 2006), Vol. 1, 466; Bartra, *Regeneración 1900–1918*, 31; Hedda Garza, *Latinas: Hispanic Women in the United States*, 2nd ed. (Albuquerque: University of New Mexico Press, 2001), 47. Victoriano Huerta came to power through a U.S.-sponsored coup d'état in February 1913.
10. *The New York Times* (May 10, 1911), cited in Garza, *Latinas: Hispanic Women in the United States,* 45.
11. Diane Telgin and Jim Kamp (eds.), *Notable Hispanic Women* (Detroit: Gale Research, Inc., 1993), 331; see also Garza, 45; and Ruiz and Sánchez Korrol, 465.
12. Garza, 40–41; Telgin and Kamp, 405–406; Paul Vanderwood, "Santa Teresa: Mexico's Joan of Arc," in Judith Ewell and William H. Beezley (comps.), *The Human Tradition in Latin America: The Nineteenth Century* (Wilmington: Scholarly Resources, 1989), 215–232.
13. Garza, 48; Ruiz and Sánchez Korrol, 465.
14. See Cockcroft, *Mexico's Hope*.
15. Garza's book and the following works are a small sampling of the "rescue" of the hidden or repressed history of the important role played by Mexican immigrants and the Magonistas in the formation of the working-class struggle and the fight for democracy in the United States: Rodolfo Acuña, *Occupied America* (New York: Harper & Row, 1972); Gale Ahrins (ed.), *Lucy Parsons: Writings and Speeches, 1878–1937* (Chicago: Charles H. Kerr Publishing Company, 2004);

James D. Cockcroft, *Latinos in the Making of the United States* (New York: Franklin Watts/Scholastic, 1995), *Outlaws in the Promised Land: Mexican Immigrant Workers and America's Future* (New York: Grove Weidenfeld, 1988), and his works cited in *Mexico's Hope*, 118, n. 19; Juan Gómez-Quiñones, *Mexican American Labor, 1790–1990* (Albuquerque: University of New Mexico Press, 1994); John M. Hart, *Anarchism and the Mexican Working Class, 1860–1931* (Austin: University of Texas Press, 1978); Elizabeth Martinez, *500 Years of Chicana Women's History (500 Años de la Mujer Chicana)* (New Brunswick: Rutgers University Press, 2007); Javier Torres Parés, *La revolución sin frontera: El Partido Liberal Mexicano y las relaciones entre el movimiinto obrero de Mexico y el de United States, 1900–1923* (México, D.F.: Ediciones y Distribuciones Hispánicas, 1990); Alfonso Torúa Cíinfuegos, *El Magonismo en Sonora (1906–1908): Historia de una persecución* (Hermosillo: Universidad de Sonora, 2009).

16. James D. Cockcroft, unpublished interviews conducted in October 2009 with spokespeople for the Cananea strike; see also Cockcroft, *Intellectual Precursors of the Mexican Revolution*, 135–136.
17. Ricardo Flores Magón in Bartra, *Regeneración*, 282–286.
18. Cited in Cockcroft, *Intellectual Precursors*, 197.
19. See Table 3 in Cockcroft, *Mexico's Hope*, 103. In a public lecture celebrating Mexico's bicentenary in Cuernavaca, Ross Gandy said, "Mexico has suffered 270 military interventions, the record for Latin America. Why so many? Because that country has coffee, mangos, avocados, silver, iron, copper, uranium, caoba, biodiversity, petroleum, migrants and is near the monster."
20. Cited in Bartra, 42.
21. *El Mesquite* (July-December 1990), 81–82.
22. Subcomandante Marcos, *Shadows of Tender Fury: The Letters and Comuniqués of Subcomandante Marcos and the Zapatista Army of National Liberation* (New York: Monthly Review Press, 1995), cited in Cockcroft, *Mexico's Hope*, 307. Of course, there were conditions present in 1994 and afterwards that evoked strong Zapatista positions on matters not treated by the Magonistas such as ecology, sexual preferences, or genetically modified organisms. Moreover, the influence of the original peoples has been both manifest and important. The autonomous municipalities of today's Chiapas, like those being created by other original peoples in the rest of the nation, implement traditional systems of collective decision-making.
23. *Regeneración* (January 2010), 2.
24. Rosario Ibarra, "No hay derechos humanos sin las luchas de los pue-

blos, ni éxito para la lucha popular sin defensa de los derechos humanos," *Enlace Socialista* (March 28, 2010), available at www.enlacesocialista.org.mx.

25. Jesús Torres Nuño, the Trotskyist leader of the strike and current president of the cooperative enterprise Trabajadores Democráticos de Occidente (TRADOC), expects an increase in production in 2010 from 5,000 to 20,000 tires *each day*. Author's correspondence and interviews with Jesús Torres Nuño, 2002–2010. See also James D. Cockcroft, Mario Alberto Nájera, and Jesús Torres Nuño, *Testimonio de una victoria obrera del siglo XXI, una huelga internacionalista ejemplar: la batalla de Euzkadi* (Guadalajara: Ediciones Presente y Futuro, 2008).
26. "DECLARACIÓN DEL TRIBUNAL INTERNACIONAL DE LIBERTAD SINDICAL Con base a la Resolución Final sobre la vigencia de este derecho fundamental en MÉXICO, 1° DE MAYO DE 2010," available at http://www.tribunaldelibertadsindical.blogspot.com, and James D. Cockcroft, "El Tribunal Internacional de la Libertad Sindical condena a la presidencia mexicana," *Rebelión* (November 9, 2009), available at http://www.rebelion.org/noticia.php?id=94810&titular=el-tribunal-internacional. For more international labor union news in English, see http://www.labourstart.org.
27. I prefer this concept instead of "Latin America" because it doesn't make invisible the original peoples and the African peoples but I don't use it ordinarily because, as the late Carolos Montemayor (d. 2010) once observed: "in a strict sense there have not been Indians in America. There have been peoples and there exist peoples with their own names" (*La Jornada*, March 12, 2006). The African peoples also had and still have their own names, just as do other peoples of Asia, Europe and the Middle East who live in Latin America.

CHAPTER TWO: IMPERIALISM, "FAILED STATES," NEW WARS, RESISTANCE

1. http://twitpic.com.
2. Evidence showed that Andrés Manuel López Obrador received from half a million to two million more votes than Felipe Calderón, the "official" winner by an announced margin of 0.58 percent. Protesters against the fraudulent election took over the Congress, forcing Calderón to be officially inaugurated as president in a separate room under the protection of an immense military guard. In 1988 a similar fraud occurred, where the ballots were burned and top election officials later acknowledged the fraud. According to the Secretariat of

National Defense, by mid-February 2010 half of the army, some 100,000 soldiers, was patrolling urban and rural areas. The soldiers were not defending the nation against invading armies, they were killing Mexicans. Statistics, photographs, and eyewitness reports show that the majority of the victims in this war have been innocent civilians. By mid-2010, there were more than 23,000 dead, 7,000 disappeared, and 20,000 jailed.

3. Kevin Martinez and Rafael Azul, "Mexican Torture Videos Reveal Ties with U.S. Military Contractors" (July 11, 2008), available at www.wsws.org/articles/2008/jul2008/mex-j11.shtml; Eva Gollinger, "Los asesinos al lado," *Rebelión* (December 16, 2009).
4. Reported in *La Jornada* (April 10, 2010).
5. The five corporations are Time Warner, Disney, News Corporation (of the Australian-American Rupert Murdoch), Bertelsmann (of Germany), and Viacom (ex-CBS).
6. Cited in *Correspondencia de Prensa* (February 6, 2010). Blair also said that U.S. citizens in other countries can be killed by the U.S. government, a policy later confirmed by President Obama. See http://news.antiwar.com.
7. Tariq Ali, "President of Cant," *New Left Review* (January 25, 2010). For an explanation of imperialism's use of the concept "failed state," see David Sogge, "Something Out There: State Weakness as Imperial Pretext," in Achin Vanaik (ed.), *Selling US Wars* (Northampton, MA: Olive Branch Press, 2007).
8. See Carlos Fazio, "La visita," *La Jornada* (April 5, 2010); Naomi Klein, "The Rise of Disaster Capitalism," *The Nation* (April 15, 2005); and Matt Bewig, "US Ambassador to Mexico: Who Is Carlos Pascual?" available at http://www.allgov.com/ViewNews/US_Ambassador_to_Mexico__Who_Is_Carlos_Pascual_90513.
9. Rosario Ibarra, "*No hay derechos humanos sin las luchas de los pueblos, ni éxito para la lucha popular sin defensa de los derechos humanos*," *Enlace Socialista* (March 28, 2010), available at www.enlacesocialista.org.mx.
10. Gilberto López y Rivas, *Las fuerzas armadas mexicanas a fin del milenio: los militares en la coyuntura actual* (México, D.F.: Cámara de Diputados, 1999); James D. Cockcroft, *Mexico's Hope* (New York: Monthly Review Press, 1998), 340–345.
11. See Cockcroft, 335–345. According to the United Nations Office on Drugs and Crime, 85 percent of narcotraffic profits in cocaine from South America to the United States remain in the United States. See also http://weeklynewsupdate.blogspot.com/2010/06/wnu-1038-most-cocaine-profits-stay-in.html.

12. Eva Gollinger, "EEUU planea nuevas bases militares en Brasil y Perú para contener a Venezuela," available at http://www.telesurtv.net/noticias/contexto/1852/eeuu-planea-nuevas-bases-militares-en-brasil-y-peru-para-contener-a-venezuela/. See also front-page news story in *O estado de São Paulo* (March 31, 2010).
13. Cited in Greg Grandin, "Muscling Latin America," *The Nation*, February 8, 2010. See also James D. Cockcroft, *México: Momento Histórico Decisiones 2006* (México, D.F.: Universidad Autónoma de la Ciudad de México, 2006); *Mexico's Hope*, 335–345; and "Mexico's Crisis in Context of Latin America's Challenge to Imperialism" (2006), available at www.jamescockcroft.com.
14. Gilberto López y Rivas, *Contralínea* (April 4, 2010), 176. Available at http://contralinea.info/archivo-revista/index.php/2010/04/04/plan-2030-ocupacion-integral-de-mexico/. See also Nancy Flores, "Plan México 2030: desmantelar la seguridad social," available at http://contralinea.info/archivo-revista/index.php/2010/03/14/plan-mexico-2030-desmantelar-la-seguridad-social/, and Fazio.
15. The owner is Germán Larrea, Mexico's third richest man and one of the world's wealthiest individuals. He is one of those responsible for the "accidental" death of sixty-five miners on February 19, 2006 at the Pasta de Conchos mine in Coahuila. On the day the PFP seized the Cananea mines, police forcibly removed family members of the killed miners from access to Pasta de Conchos and shortly thereafter sealed the mine so that the miners' remains and other evidence could never be retrieved. In Mexico, a country with one of the highest rates of industrial "accidents" in the world, the few union leaders who defend labor rights are often falsely accused of crimes, as in the case of Napoleón Gómez Urrutia, leader of the Sindicato de Mineros. The government illegally replaced him with a *charro* leader in 2006, and he left Mexico in 2007 to continue his leadership from Vancouver, Canada. For more information on the repression of the shrinking labor unions (now comprising less than 15 percent of the labor force), see http://www.tribunaldelibertadsindical.blogspot.com/ and http://www.labourstart.org.
16. Cf. Jorge Camil, "El narco, un Estado paralelo," *La Jornada* (April 16, 2010).
17. Jacqueline Stevens, "America's Secret ICE Castles," *The Nation* (December 16, 2009); James D. Cockcroft, "Immigration, Family Destruction and Terrorism: The US-Mexican Case of Saúl Arellano," available at www.jamescockcroft.com. For more on the immigration topic, see chapter 5.

CHAPTER THREE: UNEVEN DEVELOPMENT, POLITICAL CULTURE, CLASSES, CLIENTELISM

1. The creation of Mexico's corporatist state is described in the "State and Classes" section below.
2. Valentín Campa and Demetrio Vallejo led the railroad strike of 1958–59, which was broken by federal troops. Campa and Vallejo were imprisoned for more than a decade. Rubén Jaramillo, a veteran of Zapata's guerrilla army, was simultaneously an ordained Methodist minister and a member of the Mexican Communist Party who led a peasant revolt in Morelos and was assassinated by federal troops in 1962.
3. That war never fully ended and has been intensified during the current government's militarization of the country in the name of an unwinnable "drug war" sponsored by U.S. imperialism. See chapter 2.
4. For details, see chapter 2 and Part II, "The Era of Monopoly Capitalism," in Cockcroft, *Mexico's Hope* (New York: Monthly Review Press, 1998).
5. This interpretation of the Mexican Revolution is presented with more detail in Cockcroft, *Mexico's Hope.* For other interpretations, see Héctor Aguilar Camín (comp.), *Interpretaciones de la revolución mexicana* (México, D.F.: Nueva Imagen, 1979). In the last several years a vast literature on the Revolution has expanded, refined, or supplemented earlier analyses.
6. Political scientist Gilberto López y Rivas uses the concept "transnationalized bourgeoisie" in his commentary in "Plan 2030: ocupación integral de México," Contralínea (April 4, 2010), 176; available online at http://contralinea.info/archivo-revista/index.php/2010/04/04/plan-2030-ocupacion-integral-de-mexico/. For more on Plan 2030, see chapter 2.
7. See Cockcroft, "Indigenous Peoples Rising," available at http://mrzine.monthlyreview.org/cockcroft301108.html; and "Elección presidencial en EE.UU. y escalada de injerencia en América Latina," *Rebelión* (May 17, 2008), available at http://www.rebelion.org. Venezuela's revolution also has had a continental and world impact, in part because of its thousands of local community councils that, with varying degrees of success, "govern from the bottom up."
8. For a discussion of revitalization movements, popular culture, and ideology with anthropological references, see Cockcroft, "Coercion and Ideology in Mexican Politics," in Cockcroft, André Gunder Frank and Dale L. Johnson, *Dependence and Underdevelopment: Latin America's Political Economy* (New York: Anchor Books, 1972),

245–267; and Nora Hamilton and Timothy F. Harding (eds.), *Modern Mexico: State, Economy, and Social Conflict* (Los Angeles: Sage Publications, 1986).

9. The Científicos in the cabinets of the governments of Porfirio Díaz championed U.S. and European methods of education and industrialization. Their power was very similar to that of the new "technocrats" in the era of neoliberal capitalism, with the difference of their not becoming presidents of the nation. The books and articles by Nora Hamilton and dozens of other researchers document such continuity quite well. See, for example, Hamilton, *The Limits of State Autonomy: Post Revolutionary Mexico* (Princeton University Press, 1982) and *Mexican Transitions: Contemporary Challenges, Lasting Legacies* (Oxford University Press, 2010). See also the previous footnote and James D. Cockcroft, *El Imperialismo, la Lucha de Clases y el estado en México* (México: Editorial Nuestro Tiempo, 1979), *Mexico: Class Formation, Capital Accumulation, and the State* (New York: Monthly Review Press, 1983, revised ed., 1990), and *México's Hope*.

10. Traditionally, scholars often called the production of labor power "reproduction," easily confused with "reproduction of the species." This naturalizing of a *socially constructed relationship* has been challenged in recent feminist analyses. I have benefitted from these analyses and from my discussions with Dr. Susan Caldwell. For more details on the important role of women in Mexican history, especially their contributions to popular struggles against oppression, see Cockcroft, *Mexico's Hope*.

11. Antonio Gramsci, *Selections from the Prison Notebooks* (New York: International Publishers, 1971).

12. Article 27 provides for agrarian reform, including restoration of *ejidos* to communities that originally possessed them; the nation's control over natural resources; and the right of the nation "to impose on private property such limitations as the public interest may demand." Article 123 declares that every business enterprise must share its profits with the workers and must maintain a minimum salary able to satisfy the needs of a family. Article 3 provides for free and obligatory public education.

13. The Zapatistas also championed the redemptive qualities of the Virgin of Guadalupe. They wore her image on their hats when they seized the haciendas and sugar mills in Morelos. For more on the Cristero Revolt, see David C. Bailey, *Viva Cristo Rey! The Cristero Rebellion and the Church-State Conflict in Mexico* (Austin: University of Texas Press, 1974).

14. In Latin American politics, a *caudillo* is a strong regional leader or military strongman who sometimes achieves national power.
15. Francisco Valdés Ugalde, *Autonomía y legitimidad: los empresarios, la política y el estado en México* (México, D.F.: Siglo Veintiuno Editores, 1997), 116.
16. In January 1932, the head of the U.S. Department of Agriculture had to rush to the aid of U.S. employers of Mexican immigrants in agriculture, mining, and industry by publicly declaring: "We have depended upon these people; they are not a social burden but honest men and workers who have helped so much to develop this country." Cited in Cockcroft, *Mexico's Hope*, 120–121.
17. The CGOCM was soon rebaptized the Confederación de Trabajadores Mexicanos (CTM) and in 1936 became the national labor confederation officially recognized by the government. It had 3,000 unions and 600,000 workers. Today, because of its long record of cooperation with its state sponsors and the bourgeoisie, its violent *charrismo*, and workers' struggles for trade union democracy, the CTM lacks the popularity it enjoyed in the mid-1930s and is in decline. Nonetheless, it continues its power among several important unions and the state (in the PRI sector of the state and even part of the PAN sector). In April 2010 it took a position in support of the fired electrical workers and came out against President Calderón's ultrareactionary "labor reform," opting instead for the PRI's more moderate version.
18. "Corporatism" is employed here to describe a political system that relies for its legitimacy and perpetuation on what Arnaldo Córdova has called "a politics of masses." (See Córdova, "*El desafío de la izquierda mexicana*," *Nexos* (June 1979), 3–15.) This happens when the capitalist state provides modest concessions to popular movements and ties their mass organizations to its tutelage; those who resist such incorporation are usually repressed by state force. There is considerable theoretical confusion about "populism." Most analysts agree that populism is a "something for everyone" approach but fail to distinguish its three overlapping dimensions: 1) ideology; 2) class alliances; and 3) social movement (that is, ideological and political practice of a class or group alliance). Populism is always geared toward specific class or group ends. The proletariat, for example, uses it to win reforms or even class hegemony through revolutionary changes, while the bourgeoisie or an ascendant bourgeois fraction uses it to maintain or gain hegemony and to limit proletarian demands to reforms instead of revolution. Populism *as an ideology* has existed in Mexico and many other countries for a very long time. So when

analysts like sociologist Ernesto Laclau perceive populism primarily or solely in its ideological dimension, the concept loses its historical specificity of class, class alliances, and social movement. For my critique of Laclau, see *Mexico's Hope*, 137–138.

19. Such a hegemonic project normally takes form in times of crisis, often during a transition from one stage of economic development to another; also, during a period of political transition (itself related to economic change). In the course of a given crisis, a particular class or class fraction (often the ascendant one) attempts to carry through the the transition and the class goals it seeks through ideological combat, alliance building, and other forms of political struggle. The aim of the project is to gain dominance over the state and its ideological apparatuses, to transform the state in correpsonding ways, and to subordinate or defeat rival projects and the class interests behind them—in sum, to alter the balance of power in society as a whole.
20. In reaction to the growing intensity of the class war, the state had implemented parts of the progressive program of Cárdenas *before* his inauguration, for example a minimum wage and a constitutional reform that made public education "socialist." The one consistent ideological theme of the Cárdenas administration was the creation not of a socialist regime but of a government that would be, as he so often stated, "liberal, democratic, and nationalist."
21. Friedrich Engels, letter to Danielson, June 18, 1892, cited in Hal Draper, *Karl Marx's Theory of Revolution: State and Bureaucracy* (New York: Monthly Review Press, 1977), 585.
22. During the Cárdenas government, women launched many demands, some of which were partially met, such as maternity leave for state employees, the right to vote for the national Cámara de Diputados (House of Representatives), and the right to apply for state posts.
23. Jesús Silva Herzog, interview with author, 1964, and his book, *El petróleo mexicano* (México, D.F.: Fondo de Cultura Económica, 1941).
24. Mexico eventually paid more than $200 million to the companies.
25. For statistics and details on the process of class formation and its dynamic evolution in the second half of the twentieth century, including the immiseration of millions of persons and the role of the poor in capital accumulation, see Cockcroft, *Mexico's Hope*, 194–242.
26. For a detailed explanation and several economic tables documenting the presence and influence of foreign capital, see Cockcroft, *Mexico's Hope*.
27. A minority of analysts would say that political stability lasted until 1988, when the PRI's candidate, Carlos Salinas de Gortari, lost the presidential election but, by the slimmest of margins, was declared the winner by the PRI-dominated elections board.

CHAPTER FOUR: NEOLIBERAL TERRORISM, IMMISERATION, DESTRUCTION OF FAMILIES

1. We live in a world situation that threatens us with many dangers that put at risk the survival of billions of people, entire countries, and the planet itself. These dangers have their roots in the expansion of control over our lives by the capitalist economic system and its imperialisms; its consumerist, sexist, and racist cultures; its globo-colonization; and its neoliberal economic model. The most aggressive and dangerous imperialism is the U.S. one, intent on making itself the only superpower of a so-called uni-polar world by using its military might to grab control of the markets and natural resources of the planet.
2. For years in the Andean countries (and in Cuba in the case of dengue fever) the U.S. government has been carrying out bioterrorism against peasants cultivating coca and other crops. "The National Security Strategy of the United States of America," presented in September 2002, included the possibility of directing biological weapons or a toxic virus at specific genotypes, for example Arabs, African Americans, Latinos, or any group the U.S. authorities wished to attack. It's not for nothing that the U.S. government has denied entry for international inspectors investigating the possible presence of biochemical weapons outlawed by international treaties since the end of the 1960s. The most complete documentation and history of state terrorism as a fundamental tool of U.S. imperialism is "Terrorismo Made in USA en las Américas. Una enciclopedia básica," available at www.terrorfileonline.net.
3. This is analyzed in this book's second chapter.
4. It is important to note that U.S. imperialism has a highly political character. The largest corporations and banks are well integrated with the state and the two main political parties. The state, in its search for political hegemony, is heavily immersed in international political and economic institutions such as the UN and the IMF, the World Bank, and the Inter-American Development Bank. For this reason, and not only to grab control of petroleum, the United States has launched wars in so many parts of the world—to affirm its military, economic, and political hegemony over imperialist rivals in Europe and Japan. In the words of an official U.S. government document that circulated by Internet in September 2002, "The goal of the National Security Strategy of United States of America is global and infinite in scope, designed to establish complete spectrum rule through the use of preventive war." See "The National Security Strategy of the United States of America" (September 2002), available at http://www.whitehouse.gov/nsc/nssall.html.

5. Veronika Bennholdt-Thomsen, "Investition in die Armen. Zur Entwicklungsstrategie der Weltbank," *Lateinamerika, Analysen und Berichte*, no. 4 (1980), cited in Cockcroft, *Mexico's Hope* (New York: Monthly Review Press, 1998), 208.
6. Superexploitation, as Marx pointed out, is the reduction of wages below the value of labor power (the costs necessary for workers to maintain themselves and their families), and "transforms, within certain limits, the laborer's necessary consumption fund into a fund for the accumulation of capital." See Karl Marx, *Capital*, Vol. I (New York: International Publishers, 1967), 599.
7. See chapter 3.
8. The growth of the economy's "informal sector" and the supposed "new international division of labor" is an old process deriving from imperialism's creation and distribution of the "relative surplus population," or surplus labor force, on an international scale. National wage differentials have to do, in part, with the power advantages that imperialist nations have accumulated in the course of time. From that historical evolution of imperialism there thus developed the concepts of the "new international division of labor" and "the need to be competitive in the global market," used by transnational corporations and their spokespeople to extend even further their accumulation of capital. Famed Mexican economic historian Sergio de la Peña long ago pointed out that the capitalist mode of production "wherever it spreads, absorbs other modes of production" rather than coexisting with them. See de la Peña, "Acumulación originaria y el fin de los modos de producción no-capitalistas en América Latina," *Historia y Sociedad*, no. 5 (Spring 1975), 65–73. See also Jorge Alonso et al., *Lucha urbana y acumulación de capital* (México, D.F.: Ediciones de la Casa Chata, 1980); José Antonio Alonso, *Las costureras domésticas de Netzahualcóyotl* (Puebla: Universidad Autónoma de Puebla, 1981). See also Cockcroft, "Pauperización urbana y rural," *Coyoacán* 15 (January-June, 1983), 25–64; "Immiseration, Not Marginalization," *Latin American Perspectives*, Vol. X, Nos. 2 and 3 (Spring/Summer 1983), 86–107; *Mexico's Hope*, 194–242; and the final part of the section "State and Class" in chapter 3.
9. Marx, *Capital*, Vol. I (New York: International Publishers, 1967), 633, 644–645.
10. Cited in *Correspondencia de Prensa* (March 10, 2001). I have altered slightly an English translation I found at http://www.imow.org.
11. For this commentary on the family and the state I have benefitted much from conversations with Dr. Susan Caldwell.
12. Guillermo Bonfil Batalla, *Mexico Profundo, una civilización negada* (México, D.F.: CIESAS/SEP, 1987).

13. In 2007, the UN passed its Declaration of Rights of Indigenous Peoples, with only four "No" votes (United States, Canada, Australia, and New Zealand; the last two have since renounced their votes and signed the Declaration). It echoed and expanded the ILO's Convention 169 on Indigenous and Tribal Peoples that entered into force in 1991.
14. For analyses of the indigenous problematic and contemporary Zapatismo in more detail see Cockcroft, *México: Momento Histórico Decisiones 2006* (México, D.F.: Universidad Autónoma de la Ciudad de Mexico, 2006) and *Mexico's Hope*, 196–206, 302–335; Héctor Díaz-Polanco, *La rebelión zapatista y la autonomía* (México, D.F.: Siglo Veintiuno Editores, 1997); Paulina Fernández C., "Gobierno autónomo zapatista Características antisistema político mexicano" (February 15, 2010), available at http://enlacezapatista.ezln.org.mx; and Leo Gabriel and Gilberto López y Rivas, *El universo autonómico: propuesta para una nueva democracia* (México, D.F.: UAM-Plaza y Valdés, 2008).
15. Gilberto López y Rivas, "Tesis en torno a la autonomía de los pueblos indios," *Rebelión* (May 29, 2010).
16. Ibid.
17. This is analyzed in chapter 3.
18. For pioneering feminist works behind this conceptualization, see Wally Seccombe, *A Millennium of Family Change: Feudalism to Capitalism in Northwestern Europe* (New York: Verso, 1992) and *Weathering the Storm: Working-Class Families from the Industrial Revolution to the Fertility Decline* (New York: Verso, 1993). There is an abundant literature on Mexican and Latin American machismo, most of which overlooks its roots in European patriarchy. For more on these themes, see Cockcroft, *Mexico's Hope*, 12–13, 146–151, and Hedda Garza, *Latinas: Hispanic Women in the United States*, 2nd ed. (Albuquerque: University of New Mexico Press, 2001), 14–16. Another important aspect of Mexican machismo is *marianismo*, or exaggerated adoration of the figure of "Mary," as in the case of the Virgin of Guadalupe who in some way is to be seen as the ultimate representation of the good and the pure, as well as the savior of humanity. Under patriarchy, women are expected to "live up to" this demanding ideal.
19. *Mexican Labor News Analysis*, vol. 3, Special Issue: International Women's Day (March 1998), available at www.ueinternational.org. Much of the information on women in this section is elaborated there. See also Cockcroft, "Gendered Class Analysis: Internationalizing, Feminizing, and Latinizing Labor's Struggle in the Americas," *Latin American Perspectives*, Issue 103, 25: 6 (November 1998), 42–46.

20. Héctor de la Cueva, "1 de Mayo de 2010: en riesgo todos los derechos laborales," *Correo Laboral cilas* (April–May 2010), 4–5; available at http://www.tribunaldelibertadsindical.blogspot.com. See also chapters 1 and 2 of this book. Among the many thousands who have formed independent unions are nuclear industry workers, telephone workers, electrical workers, miners, pilots, university workers, schoolteachers, and a fourth of the petroleum industry's workforce.
21. The commune of Oaxaca was a participatory and just democracy from below that inspired millions of people in the rest of Mexico and in other parts of the world but was crushed in 2006 by federal troops, the Federal Preventive Police (PFP), and death squads responsible for twenty assassinations. It suffered internal divisions afterwards.
22. http://coalitionforjustice.info.
23. For details on the history of the "new" labor militancy, see Cockcroft, *Mexico's Hope*, 261–356.
24. Josefina Chávez Rodríguez, "Misoginia, militares y sicarios: 17 años de pesadilla en Juárez," *Cuadernos Feministas* (February 16, 2010).
25. Article 1 of the current version of the 1917 Constitution prohibits "All types of discrimination whether it be for ethnic origin, national origin, gender, age, different capacities, social condition, health condition, religion, opinions, preferences, or civil state or any other which attacks human dignity" and Article 4 proclaims "All people, men and women, are equal under the law" and that everyone has "the right to decide, in a free, responsible and informed manner, the number and spacing of one's children."
26. I have benefitted greatly from conversations with Mexican feminist Heather Dashner Monk about the campaign for the right to free and safe abortion.
27. On the secret deal consult Michael Tangemen, *Mexico at the Crossroads: Politics, the Church and the Poor* (Maryknoll: Orbis, 1994), 69–82.
28. Roderic Ai Camp, *Cruce de espadas: política y religión en México* (México, D.F.: Siglo Vintiuno Editores, 1997), 180.
29. From the author's conversations with Dr. Ross Gandy Jordán, professor of the National Autonomous University of Mexico and collaborator of the progressive Church in Cuernavaca.
30. Javier Sicilia, "La puta casta," *Proceso* (May 26, 2010.)
31. It is now known that the founder of Legionnaires of Christ, the deceased Mexican priest Marcial Maciel, was guilty of sexual abuses that the Church covered up until 2010. An editorial in *La Jornada* (April 27, 2010) commented,"the Catholic Church has not been able to prevent the exhibition of its most scandalous institutional miseries:

the mechanisms and norms of protection for sexual abusers in the ranks of the clergy."

32. Álvaro Delgado, *El Yunque: La ultraderecha en el poder* (México, D.F.: Plaza y Janés, 2003) and *El ejército de Dios: Nuevas revelaciones sobre la extrema derecha en México* (México, D.F.: Plaza y Janés, 2005). Delgado's research contains information on the Yunque that the PRI's secret service discovered. He won the National Journalism Prize in 2003 for *El Yunque* and received several death threats.
33. "La Arquidiócesis pide el retiro del Ejército," *El Universal* (December 14, 2009), cited by Dan La Botz, "Mexico Labor Year in Review," *Mexican Labor News and Analysis* (January 2010).

CHAPTER FIVE: MIGRATION, HUMAN AND NATURE'S RIGHTS, POLITICKING, RESISTANCE

1. López Obrador, *La mafia que se adueñó de Mexico . . . y el 2012* (México, D.F.: Grijalbo, 2010), 136–137.
2. Vicky Peláez, "Despierta Inmigrante: ¡Llegó tu hora!" (April 7, 2006), available at http://ecuador.indymedia.org. Small and medium enterprises sustain 80 percent of employment in Mexico. Hundreds of thousands of them have collapsed because of competition from the North, as 6,000 Mexicans lose their jobs every day, according to Andrés Manuel López Obrador in his new book cited above
3. To read more on this problematic, see Cockcroft, *Latinos in the Making of the United States* (Danbury, CT: Franklin Watts and New York: Scholastic, 1995); *Outlaws in The Promised Land: Mexican Immigrant Workers and America's Future*, 2nd ed. (New York: Grove Weidenfeld, 1988); *Mexico's Hope* (New York: Monthly Review Press, 1998), 120–121 and 356–383; José Jacques y Medina, *De mojado a diputado, Memoria gráfica y documental* (México, D.F.: Cámara de Diputados, 2009), Marta Sánchez Sóler, *México: Hacia una Reforma Integral del Estado, Reporte acerca de la Migración y los Principales Temas que Interesan a los Migrantes mexicanos en los Estados Unidos* (México, D.F.: Instituto de Estudios de la Revolución Democrática, 2005), 435–448, and David L. Wilson and Jane Guskin, *The Politics of Immigration: Questions and Answers* (New York: Monthly Review Press, 2007).
4. See Cockcroft, "Immigration, Family Destruction and Terrorism: The U.S.-Mexican Case of Saúl Arellano," available at www.jamescockcroft.com.
5. See Tom Barry, "Community Security Mission Creep at Homeland Security," *Americas Program Policy Report* (July 10, 2009); and

Jacques y Medina, *De Mojado a Diputado*, 137–148. In this section on immigration I have benefitted greatly from conversations with José Jacques y Medina, Marta Sánchez Soler, and Elvira Arellano in Mexico, 2009–2010.

6. See Department of Homeland Security, "DHS Policy Number 11001.1 - FEA Number 601-03 – DEC. 08 2009 - U.S. Immigration and Customs Enforcement, memorandum, John Morlon, Assistant Secretary National Fugitive Operations Program: Priorities, Goals, and Expectations, and U.S. Department of Homeland Security Bureau of Immigration and Customs Enforcement, Form M-592 (8/15/03)," entitled "ENDGAME, Office of Detention and Removal Strategic Plan, 2003 - 2012, Detention and Removal Strategy for a Secure Homeland," available at http://www.ice.gov.
7. Ibid.
8. Jessica Vaughan, Center for Immigration Studies, "Attrition through Enforcement: A Cost-Effective Strategy to Shrink the Illegal Population" (April 2006), available at http://www.cis.org/articles/2006/back406.html.
9. See Justin Akers Chacón, "Who's Behind the Anti-Immigrant Crusade?" (June 11, 2010), available at http://socialistworker.org. Chacón is coauthor with Mike Davis of *No One Is Illegal: Fighting Racism and State Violence on the U.S.-Mexico Border* (Chicago: Haymarket Books, 2006). It should be noted that U.S. Census Bureau projections indicate that even without the continued immigration of "brown people" whites will become a minority by the middle of the twenty-first century.
10. See David Holthouse, "The Year in Hate," Southern Poverty Law Center Intelligence Report (Spring 2009); and Kent Paterson, "Manufacturing a Border Crisis," *Americas' Program*, available at http://www.cipamericas.org/archives/2508. Paterson notes that El Paso and San Diego are rated among the safest cities in the United States. "If we look at the data, the border is more secure now than ever before," Homeland Security Secretary Janet Napolitano recently declared.
11. Carrie Budoff Brown, "Dems' Tough New Immigration Pitch," *Politico* (June 10, 2010), available at http://www.politico.com/news/stories/0610/38342.html; National Immigrant Solidarity Network (August 10, 2010), available at http://www.ImmigrantSolidarity.org.
12. Dennis Bernstein and Jesse Strauss, "El Paso 'Cat and Mouse' Turns Fatal," *Truthout* (June 13, 2010), available at http://www.truthout.org/el-paso-cat-and-mouse-turns-fatal60391. According to Mexico's Foreign Ministry, seventeen Mexicans have been assassi-

nated or wounded in the first half of 2010 in actions related to the use of force by agents of the U.S. Border Patrol. With each new incident, declarations surface comparing the situation of the militarized border with occupied Palestine and the Gaza Strip. To justify the use of lethal force against someone who is throwing a stone, as with the "justification" of the murder of Sergio Adrián Hernández, appears absurd. See Secretaría de Relaciones Exteriores, comunicado 174 (June 8, 2010), available at www.sre.gob.mx/csocial/contenido/comunicados/2010/jun/cp_174.html.

13. For example, the percentage of women in the migratory flow increased to 40 percent in the year 2000. The flow is decreasing now because of the global economic crisis; there is less employment in the North than before. The remittances of immigrants historically maintained a significant part of the Mexican economy, but now some immigrants depend on monies sent to them by relatives and friends in Mexico.

14. The bill is reproduced in English and Spanish in Cockcroft, *Outlaws in the Promised Land*, 279–282; and in Spanish in Cockcroft, *Historia de un pueblo migrante los trabajadores de Michoacán* (México, D.F.: Jorale Editores, 2005), 117–118, and Jacques y Medina, *De mojado a diputado*, 33.

15. See José Enrique González Ruiz, *Balance de los derechos humanos en el "sexenio del cambio"* (México, D.F.: Universidad Autónoma de la Ciudad de México, 2009); and Mike Whitney, interview with Laura Carlsen, director of the Americas Policy Program in Mexico City (December 24, 2009), available at http://www.themarketoracle.biz/Article16054.html?vote2009. The United States is the only nation that has ever been condemned as a rogue state by the International Tribunal in the Hague, The Netherlands, for having committed international terrorism (Nicaragua in 1986), and that has vetoed a UN Security Council resolution calling on governments to observe international laws. In 2003, the Organization of American States (OAS) threw the United States off its Human Rights Comission. President Obama was awarded the Nobel Peace Prize, and he later sent 30,000 more U.S. soldiers to war in Afghanistan.

16. Cited by Carlos Fernández-Vega in *La Jornada* (June 16, 2010). In an editorial that same day, *La Jornada* commented that the decision in the ABC case "extended the record of disgraceful rulings" by the SCJN: "the exoneration of Puebla's governor Mario Marín [a member of the PRI, Institutional Revolutionary Party, involved with other political and business figures in child molestation networks]; the freeing of those involved in the Acteal massacre; the exoneration of those responsible for the repression in Atenco . . ."

17. See article on Cananea and López Obrador in *La Jornada*, February 12, 2010, and Rosario Ibarra, "No hay derechos humanos sin las luchas de los pueblos, ni éxito para la lucha popular sin defensa de los derechos humanos," *Enlace Socialista* (March 28, 2010), available at www.enlacesocialista.org.mx. Ibarra insists that the army must return to the barracks and that the current government "is repeating the cruel repressions of the *Priista* governments that ordered troops to repress thousands of railway workers in 1959, students in 1968, and peasant and indigenous peoples and communities in the 70s." She notes that "almost all the country is militarized with dozens of soldiers in the streets and public squares in a lost war against drugs that the Mexican people did not decide. . . . From the perspective of authoritarian power only profits count, above the lives of the citizenry."
18. According to a report in *La Jornada* (June 13, 2010), more than sixty of the hunger strikers had been sent to hospital because of their physical deterioration diagnosed by doctors. I visited the hunger strikers after the meeting with the Chief Justice, and I spoke with each one of them, women and men, to express my admiration and support. The position of the SME, in the words of its leader Martín Esparza, was "either they are judges or accomplices. . . . We will prepare ourselves for what follows. . . . Until now we have fought with the law in our hands" (cited in *La Jornada*, June 11, 2010).
19. See Russell H. Bartley, "Evidencias de un posible involucramiento de intereses foráneos en el asesinato de Manuel Buendía," *Revista mexicana de comunicación* (May–June, 1989), 11–17; and "El caso Buendía: ¿cerrado sin resolver?" *Revista mexicana de comunicación* (November–December, 1993), 12–17; Matthew Rothschild, "Who Killed Manuel Buendía? A Mexican Mystery," *The Progressive* (April 1985): 18–23; Jeff Sharlet, "Anarchist Superstar: The Revolutionary Who Filmed His Own Murder," *Rolling Stone* (January 2008).
20. See chapter 4. The list of such crimes against humanity is lengthy. To cite one of hundreds of cases insufficiently known: from July 2009 to May 2010 in a Nahua community of Ostula, Michoacán, there were eight assassinations and at least three kidnappings and forced disappearances. Moreover, federal troops frequently invaded the community. Forced sterilization continues as part of traditional ethnocide against the original peoples. The "Afro-descendant" peoples also suffer human rights violations and say that they prefer to be called by their name, "*pueblos negros*" (black peoples), and that federal authorities should recognize them in the censuses so that they might receive public services. See news stories in *La Jornada*, e.g., June 8, 2010.
21. As rural sociologist Gustavo Esteva commented in *La Jornada* (June

14, 2010): "An inevitable comparison has been made between the San Juan Copala events and what happened to the freedom flotilla that tried to break the siege of Gaza." The repression in Oaxaca is by no means the first time that human rights activists have been attacked in Mexico and the authorities have not punished the offenders. Perhaps the best known case is the extrajudicial execution in 2001 of the prominent human rights lawyer Digna Ochoa y Placido. See Linda Diebel, *Betrayed: The Assassination of Digna Ochoa* (New York: Carroll and Graf Publishers, 2007).

22. Miguel Concha, "Daños colaterales," *La Jornada* (June 12, 2010).
23. For understanding in more depth the situation of youth, I have benefitted from my frequent conversations with publisher Jorge Cleto.
24. See Lamberto González Ruiz, "Derechos humanos laborales," in José Enrique González Ruiz, *Balance*, 309–325.
25. Many scientists from the industrialized countries attended.
26. See http://www.movimientos.org and http://cmpcc.org/. Eighty percent of the greenhouse gases in the atmosphere that cause global warming come from the most industrialized countries, but all of humanity suffers the consequences—thus the climatic debt.
27. See "Asamblea Nacional de Afectados Ambientales advierte desastre ambiental en México" (February 2, 2010), available at http://www.kaosenlared.net/noticia/asamblea-nacional-afectados-ambientales-advierte-desastre-ambiental-me, and in English at www.americaspolicy.org; González Ruiz, *Balance*, 343–377.
28. See editorial in *La Jornada* (June 9, 2010).
29. Gilberto López y Rivas, in *Contralínea* 176 (April 4, 2010), http://contralinea.info/archivo-revista/index.php/2010/04/04/plan-2030-ocupacion-integral-de-mexico/.
30. See Cockcroft, "La crisis de México en el contexto del desafío de América Latina al imperialismo," *Rebelión*, October 13, 2006, and other articles available at www.jamescockcroft.com, and *México: momento histórico. Decisiones 2006* (México, D.F.: Universidad Autónoma de la Ciudad de México, 2006).
31. There are some Zapatista youth who have criticized a bureaucratic tendency in the Zapatista movement. For more information on the political parties, social movements, and guerrilla groups in the last forty years (and before), see Cockcroft, "La crisis de Mexico," *Mexico's Hope*, and *México: momento histórico.*
32. López Obrador, *La mafia que se adueñó de Mexico . . . y el 2012* (México, D.F.: Grijalbo, 2010), 191 and 205.
33. The quotes from López Obrador are in the Mexican press, for example, *La Jornada*, June 14, 2010, and April 10, 2010, and his book.

For a critique of the IFE and TEPJF and proofs of the electoral fraud of 2006, see José Antonio Crespo, *2006 hablan las actas: Las debilidades de la autoridad electoral mexicana* (México D.F.: Debate, 2008). The workers at the IFE have been prohibited from forming a union, another violation of trade union freedom in Mexico.

34. See the editorial in *Regeneración* (June 2010); López Obrador, 24, 29, 56–59; Octavio Rodríguez Araujo, "The Emergence and Entrenchment of a New Political Regime in Mexico," *Latin American Perspectives* (January 2010), 35–61.
35. Marco Rascón, "Pricentenario," *La Jornada* (April 27, 2010).
36. The list of militant rural and urban organizations is far too long to reproduce here, but includes: Barzón Popular (consisting of small farmers and businesspeople); Movimiento Urbano Popular-Frente Nacional del Movimiento Urbano Popular (MUP-FNAMUP); Asociación Nacional de Abogados Democráticos (ANAD) (National Association of Democratic Lawyers); Asociación Nacional de Empresarios Independientes (independent businesspeople); the Centro para el Desarrollo Integral de la Mujer (CDIM, pro-women's rights); Corriente Clasista de Trabajadores (a radical workers' current); the Central Campesina Cardenista (one of many recently formed peasant organizations); the student group Contracorriente; the Federación de Estudiantes Campesinos Socialistas de México (socialist peasant students); the Red Ciudadana de no Violencia y Dignidad Humana (a pacifist citizens' network); the Alianza Mexicana por la autodetermination de los Pueblos (a broad coalition for self-determination); the Movimiento por la Soberanía Alimentaria y Energética, los Derechos de los Trabajadores y las Libertades Democráticas (food and energy sovereignty, workers' rights and democracy); the Alianza de Trabajadores de la Salud y Empleados Públicos (health workers and public employees); and on and on.
37. For examples, see Cockcroft, *México: momento histórico*.
38. Cited in *La Jornada* (June 8, 2010). In 2005 Cananea's workers supported USW members in Arizona on strike against Asarco, another mining enterprise of Grupo México (see chapter 2).
39. The OAS also has found Mexico in violation of labor rights. Experts say that the ILO cannot pronounce on the violent "administrative dissolution" of the Central Light and Power Company (LyFC) since it is a prerogative of the Mexican government but that the ILO can issue a judgment on the manner in which the LyFC was dissolved. On July 9, 2010, the Federal District's Superior Court of Justice invalidated the trumped-up corruption charges and dismissed the arrest warrant against Miners' Union leader Napoleón Gómez Urrutia. Then, in

early August 2010, a Sonoran district judge ruled in favor of the Cananea miners' *amparo*, provisionally suspending the effects of the government's repressive actions and ordering the immediate removal of the PFP (Federal Preventive Police) and scabs from Cananea's mines, the reinstatement of the union's workers, and recognition of their strike. At least twenty accidents had already injured the scabs, verifying the miners' claims of unsafe conditions that gave rise to their strike in the first place.

40. For the full text of Trumka's speech, see http://downwithtyranny.blogspot.com.
41. The International Tribunal of Conscience of Peoples in Movement has its roots among pro-immigrant activists all over the world who in October 2010 celebrate the Fourth World Social Forum of Migrations in Quito, Ecuador (see http://www.fsmm2010.ec), and on November 7 and 8 in Mexico City participate in the Third International Assembly of Migrants, Refugees and Displaced Persons, sponsored by the International Migrant Alliance (see http://tribunalmigrante.saltoscuanticos.org/?p=235).

CONCLUSION: REACTIVATE THE REVOLUTIONARY FIGHT!

1. Speech upon arrival in Mexico City concluding the "Marcha del Color de la Tierra" (March of the Color of Earth) reported widely in the press.
2. Obrador, *La mafia que se adueñó de México . . . y el 2012* (Mexico: Grijalbo, 2010), 57.
3. See Cockcroft, "Uneven and Combined Development: Mexico's Crisis in Historical Context," *Against the Current* (September–October 2010), and "Mexico: 'Failed States,' New Wars, Resistance," *Monthly Review* (November 2010). Mexico's *maquiladoras* have not been able to compete with Chinese exports.
4. Early examples of this "distancing" were Secretary of State Hillary Clinton's acknowledgment that "we are nowhere near what I would consider an effective strategy" in the war against drugs (cited in *La Jornada* , May 13, 2010) and U.S. ambassador Carlos Pascual's oft-repeated statement that "the violence generated by organized crime can cause businesses to no longer consider investing in Mexico" (see, for example, *Associated Press*, April 22, 2010).
5. The transitional demands are the following: respect for the Constitution, the laws, and human and labor rights for all; respect for trade union autonomy and elimination of the corporativist system;

constitutional protection of the universal right to have free water; budgetary hikes for education, science, and culture; universal medical service and social security; solution of environmental problems; "no" to privatization and "yes" to deprivatization; food sovereignty and eradication of poverty; an end to impunity, militarization, assassinations, and tortures; freedom for political prisoners and punishment for violators of human rights; a judicial political trial of Calderón; democratic participation of all the peoples that includes the right to call a referendum and to remove officials by popular vote; renegotiation or elimination of NAFTA; economic democracy based on social solidarity that includes reactivation of the domestic market, programs for industrial and agrarian development, the *ejido* and the right to land, new banks, and transparency of federal resources; democratization of the media; a nonmilitary and social solution to the narcotrafficking problem that could radically reduce the profits and crimes if it included legalization of marijuana in the United States.

6. Andrés Manuel López Obrador, *La mafia*, 140.
7. Entrevista con Adolfo Gilly, *Correspondencia de Prensa* (May 24, 2010).
8. Carlos Fazio has written that de facto President Calderón "has tried to transform fear into a form of social control." See *La Jornada* (May 3, 2010).
9. Cited in *La Jornada*, May 3, 2010.
10. "Patriotic" in the sense defined by Cuba's voice of national independence, José Martí: "*patria es humanidad*" (fatherland is humanity). Article 129 of Mexico's Constitution says that "no military authority may, in time of peace, perform any functions other than those that are directly connected with military affairs." Calderón has violated that article since the first days of his administration, during which he substantially increased the salaries of the military and federal police and sent them, in a time of peace, into the streets and countryside supposedly to open fire on the narcos but, as we have seen, in practice to blow away civilians in what his government classifies as "collateral damage." Calderón boasts of having expanded the police force from 6,000 to 33,000. Mexico has 250,000 troops in its armed forces.
11. See Nancy Fraser, "Feminism, Capitalism and the Cunning of History," *New Left Review* (March–April 2009).
12. The media are engines of injustice against which we have to fight every day. The "battle of ideas" includes not only the creation and use of alternative means of communication but also demands for the democratization of the actually existing media.

13. See Michael Löwy, "Ni calco ni copia: Che Guevara en búsqueda de un nuevo socialismo," available at http://www.nodo50.org/cubasigloXXI/congreso/lowy_10abr03.pdf.
14. There already are international discussions taking place among activists all over the world on the themes mentioned here, including the ideas of forming a permanent national front of parties, social movements, and international networks—a "Fifth International."

Index